Typo

By Frances Tara Stirling Home Drummond Moray

To

I love you

AuthorCraft

Published by
AuthorCraft Ltd
16, Croydon Road,
Waddon, Croydon, Surrey CR0 4PA

www.authorcraft.co.uk
+44(0)20 8688 2598

ISBN 978-1-910125-94-6

Printed by IngramSpark

About the Author

Frances lives in Perthshire and has met lots of people once, including Leonardo Di Caprio. She studied criminology, philosophy, history and history of art at Edinburgh University. She hopes this 40 year old bi polar book will give her another upwardly mobile holiday. She likes getting engaged, interior design, painting, photography, Roald Dahl, Monty Python and recycling.

This book is for you if you've ever wondered what magic is.
The author once completed The Tour de France when she beat Lance Armstrong with a milkshake. There are autistic and PTSD elements.
This book was written after a dream about Alan Bennett

1

Dunk is square to what I want him to be, Dunk is a bloke I met again and again. Dunk is a tramp with his clothes and his hair. Dunk is a tank, an HGV and a plank, a two deck lorry of shiny cars, a skip that sits outside my door. Dunk lives in a glass with the window open, he sings about folk and times to curfew. There are people about who stand in wings keeping choke for admiration. Dunk is my dad and plays the saxophone like President Clinton. In the early years he waged his legs in beer like Mr. Bandy knows Guinness and rhyme. It became the stage of barley and rum to think that teeth were pairs of trousers clang to the gong. There are concerts all over Britain where Dunk makes pastry for pleasure that no-one understands. He drawls fast words about an island where clover and whisky are the same shade of green. In days of yore, there is a score and that's what daffodils and posies grow from. Not all tramps live in the hedge, but that's where I met Dunk. He was all settled beneath leaves of lime, like St. Francis of Assisi, one s short of Mississippi, holding a microphone made of crocuses. He didn't say much about the verge but there were goldfish in nearby puddles that burbled on about Dr. Foster's departures to Gloucester. position of the verge was an exact location, like the time when Arthur found sword and when Moses walked the sea bed. It was particular to fantasy in the form of permission. trees understood that they were underhand hairstyles in the relative scheme of covering skulls cleverly. Clumps of parsley. first thing he said to me smelt like floating pinches of malt. He wore large platform shoes that were flat as the earth rounds articles. 'Let's get a deck chair' he smiled, reaching for the hollow by bluebells. He rigged up two that were made from stag antlers slung with moss, according chi Fix It. It had been a walk when Armstrong scuffed his boots on the moon but the sky is mainly rocket based, propelled by engines and re-constituted whey. From the verge, the mantle split in half as a mid month shadow makes light and dark shed nostrils. Such a place had no choice except the memory of how it would. The moss was comfortable, not queasy, wet or exceptional even in the valley. There are years by hundred when calamity makes cheese, matter is coincided. best sense of persecution is to prevent and masses of books aren't furtively read. A chameleon keeps a diary of where to tread and cover ground. Things that move have passports so they can book into B & Bs. Milk and honey come by jars of shelf life, farms to cities, galaxies book the meteoric. It was a Monday to Sunday-night at this place and bullfrogs were charming. You may be thinking Leopard and Kid, Lion and Lamb, but there were no sirens of number to hand. It was play school's window with old flake in the warm-up lounge drinking scales of coffee without the dust of spectacle. Sign language is a funny truth to square. Twinkle Toes wear brilliant shoes for tapping with their fingers. The band does sticks on drums in shanga langa lang. Touring a Claudian wood to turn by brooks, bells and Lilly petals strung to guts. Paragraphs of fancy line the motorway with Little Chefs and Granadas. There's a sign for one with twenty miles ahead, on the M six, another in twenty four. A mysterious edge is always granted for breakdown, sausages for fat, polystyrene for cups of where to go. In the story of enchantment, girls and boys play forest in Sherwood. Lassie fetches help and lassoes ring beasts of misadventure. Skirt high mothers are cloudy judges of preoccupation, small is their achievement. Big Daddies on the road hurdle bogus obstacles. The plum about Dunk is always introduction. As a character of fiction he sticks to salutation. It's like the writing on carrier bags that go everywhere without moving shop. Narnia to the wardrobe, growl to the lion, thunder to storm, tablet to commandment, boom, shake, shake, shake the room. Big Dunk of obvious from what Dunk is not primula, is not accordion, nor punk, apostrophe. Pharmaceutically, Dunk is legally bound to a shrink's metaphor. As ridiculous, Freud is entertaining, as pernicious he wears tweed. St. Francis sings the Bill of Rights from the oldest book of twitter publish aviary. It might seem that meeting up in the verge is insincere to bravery. The languish of anguish is this place of invention, streams that run up hillsides. There's an old pot soaking in the sink which has a right for cleaning. The washing up brush will sort it in a swivel swirl, and Miss Bounty will look to it again for encores in risotto. In the water babies, grains of rice flush down the sink to the brink where stones are sweets and colours rinsed. A mockery of what happens if lunch is done without applause. The kid says 'May I' to repeat a question. Commands to get down are answered in question. There is nothing special about Pot Noodle apart from convenience and whacky company. Zany affords peaches in a cup, the all in one of James Giant. It's the food of bowling alley heroics. Instruction about Water Level allows for excess. Sweet and sour is coping for choice. Distinct difference about noodles and grated cheese is that noodles preserve strings for orchestras of easy lays no cutlery. Cookery programs have methods about worth and convenience. Dried food is a marvelous bargain for Helen MacArthur and Sir Ranulph Fiennes. Absorbing the myth loves to drench a protocol factory for everyone to buy a turn. Environment of piece is tastiest hill, also the friendship of rabbits in hillsides, badgers in gardens and discoveries that marriage is an awesome chunky plot. Bit of the same loaf is toil to match speed. Some may be interested to know more about the Garden of Paradise, based as it is on secrets. Some look to the motorway with interest, to Hull on how to cast an anchor. Miniature kitchen of arms and legs will dish out cookery, how to shop and what expression to wear. Avoids capture. Pot noodlers exalted as hearts of preparation. Dunk of what is and isn't there has biscuits shearing. Wooly mammoth gagging with shame for appearing. How shorn might look, and what people do in jumpers. Romantic lead does tenderness to perfection. Learned it at the RSC calls heart strings. Script even learns more than you do. Sit watch and clap mend the interval. So much practice listen with more ears. Thank God is a tingle. Oh dear is a wow. Breezes and hymns, but ultimately, force is a nice cream man that won't complain. Illustration more to the art. Stop's penance talk Hogarth. Tell me sir, Why should after this fashion. Breakfast does before eleven. There's a thing called Watchdog that measures Customer Service. What went wrong in culinary footwear. Sticky iron in dodgy boaster. After many years of living on the street, Mrs Live knows compartments. Knows how to vent in the public interest of her own life. Sometimes it's kind to give a dog a bone. Dunk knows where the labyrinth is. Mrs Live plugs in her Hoover and the dog forgets to roam. Roam and Labyrinth both explore trodden in. Dunk never treads in anything he can't get out of. At least Mrs. Live has a whistle and a dust bag. For that she is responsible. Thankful MAZDA for high price bargains. Dunk beats the carpet and lets Mrs. Live do the shake and vac. Lorry sized Kansas. Dunk fits the speed machine by vote. Today is brass haddocks for an argonaut on the hill. Today is election to go where I shall. Roman road RSC, an AA map from A to Z. Kingdom follow with interest, some read soil by square. People in the eye of the picture all end up in Dunk's Sherwood leaving their sandwich packets as proof. They may not be after Dunk specifically, for each town of man remembers. Forest hum of bees. Dunk's metaphor for fatherland supremely singled out as parent. Two nostril metaphor. Preside casual fame with keener breath than Mr's Live's suction. Painting is a sky that shelters carrots and motor ways, mountains and municipalities. Sky see in the dark earth. Water limit keep dry in touch. Okay, so it's been qualified that Dunk is hard to find directly and pin down. Joined up words of slippery jelly. Better handling than command. Toffee airplane in that write message in loops. Woops mistake for Mr. Allen. First played at the orphanage, about to end the road. Granny switch and home swaddle;

outward bound. Nativity prescribe angel suited halo of learning a catch in frisbee. Wouldn't do to swallow a lie. Name poetry drum to lady in pearls. Sword sharp as doll. Welcome home jig with animals. Crocodiles from Australian times. Disclose portions near the lobe. Men chase bashful now. Against always religion. Nature of conditional care has a few likes. Call for assembly in problems shared for profits in gold bars. Horses clop and dogs bark as man neglects and cares. Watchful upon obedience. Little children out of danger. tell them same. Some kind of body why insolence sleeps around. Convictions on tomorrow's plans not prophecy. Help stock a fridge and swallow customers. Policy derive that jeopardy is not as cool as stopping. Some like it hot as Tennessee, fetch a Sampras ball. Stop learned returned. Caesar says 'done' at a citizen deranged for leaving slaves. Policy meets dietary requirements in salads served all over the place. It is better to eat Caesar. Long time captive, not yet a slave. Read without confrontation. Language of position. Superlative and guest landscapes don't bother about packets or conscience. 'Oh, so this is Hawaii, the way a steeple brought up gravity'. Barabas is pleased by what he can learn, may not be called and so he may. May passing rights of spring. Passed off as a bore for sheep with matted coats. Thistles what he's kept for. Moults with a U because he sees Englishness. Informative comprehension of but. Significant stress as deliberate. Homework is a complete struggle for significant numbers of people. Tamed becomes idle as uncontrollable. Cost is borne in country, privately or publicly. Barabus knows what he conveys as a mixed education. Science Mr. Jam goes nowhere more than SPAM. Physics could be health. Maths is good because nobody else knows disownment cultivates skill. Up Yours off the third finger. Barabas counts for sneezing. Less complex becomes a useful tool for Caesar's countless sheep. Caesar in modern times is Ceacescu. Bless you His chapter isn't meant to be personal. Not set to meet the glass slipper. Infamy mass behaves at one frontier. E fits right and left. Slash enormously as medians. Barbarus happens as super subjections. Arrives to be persuaded to change ways. Share squatters simply sent home. Not allowed to look behind being mute, cardinal rule chocolate. Fixated by overrated temptations and force of habit to out do what can't be gone through. Take up dimness for snacks. Many of the worst people have sweet greed which permits them to underrate. Option of complex avarice going on about puddings keeping tidy. Barbie doll is what Barbaras could untie. Skins of plastic fit let the side down. Wrap peel with Wots that bit. Best plastic surgeon could have been easy to pull. Insistence to bodge and check the radio. Tune abandoned. Sliver stake for picking at the capital. Bogata wind ups are gentler as reflections. Feeling conclusions set jellies with cream. Situation overdraft exclusion. Recovery comply rulings of fortune. Negative equity suits press the buck and dine on hay, unrequited love. Who am verbatum. So far music is on the mind as dolphins are bananas. Let's be friends a thief for good conversation. Friend return return religion. Accountancy sharp reminder to see the Lord. TV list out of touch.

Wait spot the arse and feel complacent. Rat say parrot for squeak. Hand say hand the point. Diary a trace of behaviour. Sound delay parrot and rat board boat. Saint say less than crafted bloat. Lap thorough chortles. Cackle not satchel. Cheap cockles on shore. Realistic agree with mediocre reference, place passed off as a valued institution. Journalism without paper, stronger for bothering. Informed choice let them be.

How it is to know, know no is. Untoward goes away. Buffalo sense. Perpetual suns grass, bare and strewn, short and lush, luck long and rustled, content with being eaten, trodden. Public speaking is the art may take offense, capital made to defend the smell for what it is. Drains, stunk to be blocked, bad to the hat's nose, methods of efficiency. Talked about guttered. Ingenious intermittent rhythms. Keeping dry overhead. Down from the sky rooved, leaved, plocked and jittered, sobbed, sopped, mushed, wheedled, creviced, slunk, shed, ker-plunked, sheeted, mist itself, treated, crooned to split, swooned to lip, clip, pat, plitter plat splat, tinkle periwinkle, urchin moss, seaweed, somehow not lost. Sieve meet comb torn for wet when pigeon. Toes the stilts. Down and along the paddy foot. Down and flamenco pinks to clear mud, leg in sand. Don't tell anyone I toed you sir, don't spit a word, don't cheep a bird. Foot for a bargain, beak splay, tongue for toe, but don't spit forks. Up side eat levitation, palm off table. Turn up to catch. Times Chimes. dick-ory-dock mouse rang up the clock. Mouse ran down A lobotomy. Denim jacket a lemon, nothing to declare. Love from yours in faith because all options have spaces. New page begin with posting lost cow boys. Thought it was over. Paxo stuffing pesto sauce. A spot in the channel, sorry in the line of wee Urethra. fran klit, dinga ling a ding dong, fin flaps about the hot passage. Allergic to stuffing retribution. There's a mum. Just escalating with two goofy sons. Guilt embarrassing to think of at that wiley age. Then smiley, wiser, foolish, in love. Playing acting push and shove. Got off at stop that now. Glorified council corner. Entertain every perversion on 42nd Street. Street way back to the street. Chihuahua Extraditable. Cynical man next. Door to a slippery pole of conviction. Martin Amis has a move in. Beside himself with a rock bottom waif. Fuzzy raw version of Marlboro fags and red neck lace. Keith in the field, checking synopsis. Off without paper toweled hands. Back and befriend gay queue benchers with needy aplomb. Second half turn in the grate. Josie Lawrence wink like Kirsty MacColl. At the end, he nips off sharp just like the last time, to plod behind the lady in black velvet. Beg author's maze upon instruction. Watch telly tubbies curve compliments to felt hills in hospital illness. Little Bo Peep knows she has sheep by the way she is dressed. To that extent a clear view is guided and sung on the name. Bo

Peep a bye gone to stereotype and yellow umbrellas, props. Blindness frustrates her a bit once lost but forever faithful. True to the patter-cake, she potters about in peaceful carnage. Telly on three on four, picking up pieces of yore. If only she would look up more she would not be a rhyme. If only she could thrust a bit and coin her own sing song. choruses of children learn her verse, but she just stares with a frilly capped crook. 'Darling, the show's a marvel' chorus mating doves in waistcoats pecking gold. Bo Peep claps back at the same place and pew, just a different year and show. She has pins and needles, shows her crack, begs to differ that solemn hands can whack. Martin Amis is the Ivory Queen's messenger. Strain glance watch on beautifully delivered. Murder tied by the calm of fruit pie. Romance palatial to groin, elegant food, even mince. High order of buttering toast for Barbara Cartland. Absurdity existing Bo Peep as a pin up mag. Costume drag many years on and goon. Affair of knowing and not seeing. Parentally drag too, even fag in hand. Name dice about the page. Sequels born from rage, longing and despair. Better adjectives only called on when they get in from nursery. Everyone nursery, especially the Queen. Chicken licken sets off to see and tell 'the sky is falling down'. Central to what really entails a sprout corn. Emphasis of bumping head kissing, overdosing, crashing, aching. Chicken licken blameless size, age booked, alarmed prize. Smallest conflagration, petty consummation then bowl of jelly, angel delight. Warning bell of courtesy set minds to freight that moose is nearly trickery. But to chicken licken, the sky is falling down. Stages of man from chick hen goose are cluck dog bark, cat scratch, horse course, spiders in meeting match. Oh! the cynicism with a capital T. Exclaim run the course of a plane. Believe is stranded to a self floating log. Mild escape hot dog at the garage. Twenty four hour spring roll with dolomites and aqua libra. Mind of midnight snack. Thought went and fetched a VISA return. Stuff down in the city, some at walking distance.

Vine leaves aren't exactly what they spurned, and those surprise the bitterness. Kebab junk, but that's not me! Story the apostrophe. Edinburgh's weather is not indoors like aqua libra's whisky. This is bury territory opposite the hospital. Upstairs through the window. Neighbour diaphragm mouth. Battlemen slit front side. Breathing where it wasn't. That's the thing with breath, it follows, stops and starts. Not commanded breaking wind. Small flu chimneys for stoking grate. Oh, ember do remember gullet gull it, wind pipe pan stripe, whistle to the task. Ears pop on high pitch and from canals their jacket fix. Air and noise, air and noise. Mrs toad lives in the Hebrides where it is a very windy gale force time, sometimes zero index pine. It's the absent trees that racket along with crashing waves. How a howl turns to mend the stays of winter. Goose song, elephant's paw of tidings on the jet stream score. Exhaustive, invigorating, a thing called energy, harnessed by ribs and broccoli. James watt flickers at 2.31 am. before 2.32 as minutes spend. What they breathe in is out to creation. First breath not a count down, but the rest are. Old count downs server to store, old as last in jugs of the rest. Pass the water, move house to house. Swallows in the eaves are building mud for flowing over it. Sea anemone swim from the grasp of rock. That's about me, the NME accept on my behalf. Anger at the Lord ain't justified. Lord is where it's at coz there ain't no way to eat pastry. Share friends with the big 'ole dole queue at bounty expense. When eating alone, the first thing to prevaricate is gone. Chop a red pepper, blend marigolds and oil. Drip dry that's done for an ample dish. Things to know, and mistakes to find them. Makes 'em out of grasp. Lording sittin' above Port Augustus. Gloop Mr Pasta shells a panty line, missed opportunity daily, just a bone reminder. Avoid disappointment ignore sensitive time. Might be hurried to compensate. Fear of the truth and fear of the good ain't the same thing. Action written in words. For the most part, address is how it speaks. 'Y'all come over to my place' has bought resident throngs that simply don't live there. Monopoly is visiting. Goodness kept being overdone. Beyond reach about as safe as it can manage. Garden key handed as snakes of temptation, borders meet them. Qualify sliver quickly, foot on the ball. Shatter the dream jam jars. Sound sweeping away, blinking to noiseless to proudness it surveys. Particle sleeping dust corners to the eye. Half past ten line dry. There ain't nothin' busier than blinking, courage, cowardice, fighting, flirting. Game time waiting. Wanted to win the running race is winner, not cheater. Race won accurately on legs in starting positions. Sport outside sorting lanes beat dinner. Little Jack Horner knows soufflés are for darlings. Prefers plums that show. Unrefined incident pucker advantage. Tract of speed stay intact. Big getaway towards the easy. Rest there slope challenged. Best Take morning, lain mutters of talking windows. All peaceful at dawn, smatterings of catching sack. Early child burble till lunch, then screams of discontent. Day increase complication, disrupt till bed. Student up by lunch, discoed from the dread. Horizon match line excitement. Pyramid of mummy kiss a camel. Step prospect always there to recommence. Small kids deflect rays, invite returns of good behaviour. Hard believe a tantrum, for that which is responsible. Pain to bear the serious inquisition. Capacity defined individuality. Peter Sellers has trained for optimum tormentor. Wild vagaries don't square to be tamed. No shape in corridors of passing power. Not known to carry the burden and ideally sooth. Case of relieving answer, case bolted. Checked and digitally secure as someone else's luggage in patrol. Wonders on. Perspective sentimental here, with boots locked in the case. Handle progression either inflame imagination. Neither settle paper. Handled with dismay for impact. Suppose paper is bark than its growl. Too refined or unrefined, wagers of trees. Book of confiscation tell confiscation. Mind about books, invention utter. Went changed in standards of print. Churns final edit. Stolen money nearly stolen mummy. 'umm' hardly an able answer, spell. Ring in Japanese by Isuzu in September, one week to live. Eat an apple, watch an apple, inside and out, eruption, volcanoes, lid replacements. Centre core may not be around. Jaw bone cheek forehead. Sit in all of them. Video flat mates. East, west and TV to forge angular line triangular, interception of crooked. Not parallel polaroid, through the falling rain, abreast of over there. Back of head 180 thighs round 360 hairs. Knee cap Raccooners, seers that fishermen. Parts and falling wide apart. Black and white photography before colour. Facial expression mouth radiation. Speculation storm. Telephone hook getting back in the car, two spaces after a word. Meaning to inhabit. box and the chest of drawers. Keep pairs of socks. Murmur, set goals of where to walk, speak Japanese. Haunt knowledge Keep chain letters in doors. Engines run seat belts. Wells of reflection. Crow bar shadow. Fetch water on a rope. Spiral wind empty trough. Frozen over paddock lift exhaustion. Man in moon from the bottom of a well. Lift the curse climb through the TV. Privacy wrinkle post box. Pony canyon made of toffee. Saturday's child fifteen miles. Life fathom pitch, anything goes. less meaning are more. Frog is bad for you, oh, but it's a favourite thing. Symbol is less slimy. Croak old men crack joke. As legs done in France, places to sit, better hop dance. Old fatso goes back to a favourite haunt; one of huge dimension. London with nobs, only there is no stop and Get out Free wasn't stamped properly on the bottom. Meant forwards necessitates backwards where it blithely trolls principles. unprincipled frog learns to grow, without pumps and modern contraptions. He must frog it to the frog from the pole to start with. Baby help the baby. Some frogs last well into sunset, frazzled and unprinced or pressed from hops to chalks. Leap spread gorge, burn, whole bun BLT with sesame. Leap heroic, squirm ham fun. Kermit Piggy all muppetty where frogs can be, but not in hanging around. Kermy and Piggit have split up, for trying to be like Mit and Iggy but getting the message wrong. Their deserve is to think backwards, walk into things less fantastic. Have to get back together. Instructions outback are bombs and guns, tons and roads, cactuses and caucuses. Hello secret remains, forgotten and ill winds. actual problem never clearly discussed, only your place or mine. Fanny test for John; learns to play late and early. Follow that bag, that cab, that mag, that tag and safety holds a stolen prize. Body language in public spaces, private thoughts and limb disgraces. Spiders legs are curby grips, nails, spiders legs and imaginative Grecian creatures. Along comes Nescafe for being untidy. Large reminders affect the small modification, pretending not to make notice as would be fake, as would no notice take. Planting trees goes by the year, and what was is more or less than last. Currently less providing the task. Doubt goes Guns Ahead for the benefit all round. Grog is a boy. Frog is a girl. The ones with curls can't stand up and real girls and boys are cautious as pups. Retrospectively, hell hath no fury. Heat is the moment of sweating it big. Brains ooze on a couch from ten years ago when Shirley left. There was a point five years ago when cricket went to bed. The locks shut down and saw to the task of why she left in a horrible mask. It was the strain of the neighbourhood, boo hood the dog, the son or whichever one. It wasn't Shirley and it wasn't the dog. It was Prince frogged Carmichael telling the slog. Telling had attracted him to Shirley and she both surveyed. in stages, the story on release did where it went. But there was a patch of cruelty on the rounded point that fetch back. So keep slack. Carmichael thought it best for Shirley if the gates remained locked. This dug at Shirley, darning web knots. Shirley's knots were as good as any bolt, but Carmichael nagged and brains slid the ooze. The old woman was a terrible worry, but no longer. Placid tells menace there's more fire to furnace. Attractive actors, symbols, protractors. Follow a game of a trip down a step. 'No 'shall be grown up, and 'Didn't' likes 'Really' to ripen adventure. experience, diversion, absconsion, desertion add diversion, absconsion, division to the way that doesn't smile. North London is terribly good at teaching. West London is terribly good at preaching goose to the chase of upset. Nothing feeling and kicking ass are jolly good balls of trash. Burper sherpa even makes ground from demeanor, and this is a wretched state of Pass. Sulk defend proper literature in the tenure of character. Difficult to sustain sulk without explanation. There may not be another opportunity says pain again. Influence of dead inspiration in the attic, all that time of flowers the good book of inversion. Revel and relish fiction where screams await the decibel. Slightly off chord a treacherous onwards where the book hits fix wilder. Drug of diss a bad edge, but there is one. What doesn't happen does it to understood. Beryl writes a book called the wrong name. Walking around is coloured cotton. It eventually goes immune. Scratch privacy on the bench of toon. So much time to shovel disguise. Decisions to scrape a living not intended. Condense milk spread. Slow catching on enlivens. Mosquitoes learn to feast by day, encroachment of season. Dissolvable house warm everything separate. Cleavers on this and scraps of that. Wander Childers slowly and never mind logs. No assertion alone, no assertion grown. Clipped weed weary to tread. Halve intention, half understood. Data protection Hood. Epicenter understand the worst command in good. Well erupted, applaud well done. Scout works out How often the tank is cleaned and optimums depend. Splinters reward mistakes as something. Top skin deep is a nice relief. Edit for Something or other John Claude Van Dam. Bite horse cribs of sucking wood. Defend grim in desperate tame. Near end of game. Monopoly call to the bored and rich. Dice the pairs the others throw. Serve patience off argument. Fact is caustic toughness. Bright excalibur. Arthur and George a fool by name. Handsome throw illicit herd. Day meant the electric moon. Nothing happens to account. Sympathy where disgust is loose. Remain beneath in giveaways do. Trust comes to candour. Be sherpa not wanted, thank whip rounds unfinished. Some grains find home's young is empty; swallowed to the host of dementia. Farther off the plot. Sherpa drop to carry and leave the break. Arrogance decline, not to let you go. How accord the glory, slip shine the track. Downwards a memory lying on the hag of a peat bog. Honey, I don't care if the pope is you or not. Stand how it was planned, and tread the bowl. Hollow channel stand a pole. Positive gloom of simple bus ride. Compare how to ride, simple as Traffic office. Chalk and Cheese to Chiswick. It starts with may not see until you see, you see. Solace shown silence, optic sense. Chivalrous risk crossroads, treaders Offense. Pound of mince and cook gets heating. Day goes faithful to last years' rehearsal. Lay out in clouds of bees. Hive mind the head in summer. Fort about flowery deed. Persuasion goes with match but incendiary flicker. Gas works of drink in liquor. By product of diversion, consumed by Saturday plunge spring. Lovely brush flips along as the product of passing in the park. Continuing round truth make sound. Eyore find a real donkey, fun for a passport, dish beneath consequence. Bread and wine, boys and girls at coming of age. Sweetness unfair well fed. Today pronouncing first wait. Fade and strangle neck in exfoliant phase. Dandruff guards of age. Proof with a document charge. Deep settlement provide grass. Top soil plough for noticeable pearl. Understand a fingerprint. Policemen sow theirs at gradient. Sieve large percentage on reflex action. True of a hundred hours. Different there they are. On the verge, picking litter or wild flowers. Highway of conscription indication. Face a lot, mystery of colluding to plot. Generally Gung Ho. Distinct feature out of bounds. Actual place no poem of ageing. Discreet barn that yawns. Place go there, just for holidays and special occasions. Welcome to and fro ordained. Sentence by suggestion, and equation win selection. Mute aboard spite. Quell perk contingent plan. Fortunate neck break a breath. Hold participation gift. Feasible cow mad. Undergone in training. Lot fall out shout.

'Please remember to tie a knot in your pajamas,
single beds are only made for 1-10
Carmen Tuten karmoun. Manger best plan about hay there ever was. Exodus assume life before belonging. Pertain defeat who are disguise. Only ten miles by the flow. Passenger eyes the sky. Shopping trip worries her parents. Steal close to a book palm. Ambiguity at the edge of the road. Bottle top spent curious Trent. Why won't the lift work, ring the government! They don't serve tea in church. disgrace bothering mirth. Snack slice. Someone announces 'Oh, yes you had one, but look what you did with it!'
'I'm afraid it's all gone, like the people in the shop stop tone.' Any benefit of last rights is a construe of reasons to planets. 'There are no stairs in space'. Girl applies looking place. Spirit command hand to foot. Conjecture touch with fads and fashions. Untimely Doggie buries bone and says here woofie woofie,
'where's my bone'. Moved out of sight and the whole town is relieved that they don't live next door to a terrible person. Whole town share responsibility. Placement of dog search interestingly. Airport Alsatians and Scruffs for that. Dog squad on what they come upon. Hang about waver sound vibration, full of various information. Room box chord in throat. Not tangible to have the pope for dinner. Big pawn book. Conversation colossal and pretty unbelievable. Destructive about what was explained one afternoon about dropping the paper clip. Good bye golden hello. Post box fondant action. Poise and stoop. Not feeling good enough in vacuum. Heresy plays prude. Onerous keep proportion in friendship. What you may not return. Encrypt selection forward. Sluttish compliment must drowned on base. Kensington of darkest trace. Bus ferries past with mighty Oh's Wells. Achieve daisy chain on highest cutting. League chartered. Survive proceed the Oxford press. Stephen King in the land of hardware. Breast fill a jug in pinafore. God in pajamas. Extraction confounds

St. Thomas. Children Thomases congratulate proof. Amuse at the scribe's hand. More about filling the lines. Absurdly fun in dull instruction. Where's the manual. Oat so simple, coconut milk, cranberry drink, raspberries, blueberries, salmon fillet, organic bananas, organic lemons, organic broccoli, crispy leaf salad, organic soft citrus. J.S Aubergine makes 22.01. forty four earns points. Back and get two locked doors in a sense of quasi deliberation. Man answer supermarket. Comment reward about spending. Confusing a crying pretense. Outward bound surveys an empty place. Memory of the very last door with standard proportion. Subtract learn walk with rope, drip and sip. Porridge glue home. Useful person get off with things. Work at doubtful. Title over description, king cope in size. Lord of mercy constriction. Venerable open strain. Enter court of same. Mercy nude nod. Generate dress morning. It's rude to turn down a holy order's invitation. Definition hung flat sand. Obstinate spot off a drum. Baronial barrel of meals. Wheels of speeding by. Knowing exchange moan groan wind drop, spec and idle mop.

Those Frenchies seek him everywhere. Is he in heaven, or is he in hell that damned elusive Pimpernel.

Keep a ground confession in Catholicism. Take bitter on form. Half moon slices of bacon. This morning everyone wants to know.

2

My dear dynamo, I am charmed with the fish cake you sent me. The manor born was not nearly as interesting. Well past the age of temperature. Ole notes of subsidy. Telephone ring for the most part. Place under the ear. Mrs Barbara Seed hasn't rung back ever since it was made known that she was remembered for her enthusiasm. Baguette more than filling. Nobody said thank the washing up. Ex director still hairy handed and really ought to be seen to. Last straw can't mend the situation, obligation all mine. Meet in Janet's bar before driving off to Malibu to play squash and nurture the old fool of second lane cars by overtaking them. Ought to be the end of sensible paces to embark on yet another job. If the Spanish sisters are to unite the rest is pointless. Wonderlands in Study, could be up for the RIB. Why on earth in under pants. Skipper with bushy tail being smart. Future brighter than program suggest. Philippine into the House of Lords on the merit of disco. Worth suspending the present scenario of income tax. Freestyle ace and stitching pretend delineation. Culminate tendency to live over the edge. Gently ruling over the fine mist of dominion pleas. Sown of common went. Tobago carried his girl over the waterfall. Not that he had fallen in drink. Sake for last Thursday, but he did recompense committing tributaries in the same way that ought. States of queue begin to go down. Bar code credit process. South winds of Loch Nagar. Hard note scowling. Dial a gut for watching. After the little hedgerow. Decided mice relieved from self appointed chroming. Elf flowers returned to their habitat. Onion left in dark patch to sit quietly and await certitude. Fish law unnoticed. Earth sausage in position. Lesbians with Sir David Worthings Brigade Against Starving. Ease past situation of complementary breakfast. Lime pool frost cakes mention a few. Fortress remain open to the public plot of Map settlement. Even blown away. Outline settlement disturb digger from office compartment. Nice day in sunshine brochure, collective. Coffee table talent for history. record todays opals as beer mats. Remarkable seance in bendy hair pins. Mention the slices of garden prose came to a Fly storm sent by Hades who, in a fury of telephone bills, sought to end mere delectation of harmony quests with plain assertions that bicycle routes are for driving. 9pm. Last time we said that time was up was first, third, fourth and fifth senses all at once. Previous page on the second line of book making. Could return to finish a late session. Jaw construction might never have ended. First, last second and instinctive. Weekend driven saliva of the Lion gate may be observed mutually. Feint sundial survey coast of five o'clock. Area left to do, motion for the order of the week. Puzzle slouch shoulder of singular bean. Although I would so much rather have my own tongue for the gesture as it ought to have unfurled in the deep swimming pool of the visit to the toilets in the zoo. Farce of all yesterdays wasn't enough, there goes skinny waist with shins which reminds me of splinters and tall stair cases, scenes of intermediate berets, resist French Latino lift shaft for giraffes in capture. Long may they roam. Dizzy height wanting to remove that ruddy step ladder from out behind the marble toilet should be considered, should be full on the rung of all chains. As upon a monkey stool, some chimpanzees never listen but with congregation. For in the passing of sitting next to verity, construction bridges European. Box wake Finnegan. Recompense to love it. Weather spit off drop disease. Release nodes. Hitch and hoe, jump toe. Sow old keen stream of new born dairy lee. Went for it. baked for the old bit. Custard slow old green for dynamite that might have been practiced. Residency would not know that this continual assessment is not only boring to the fan club show of doing another episode, but that a boring life of yes to your particular sort of agreement is the westerly sense of going about and minding ones own business. Should any ball miss the anticipate heel it alternates keel and grabs the handrail. goes up and down and along the floatcake of wedding Super Nova. Charities upon us, effort shower played Paterson with inner drops of ever supposing. Soap stone pockets lightly covered by knuckle dusters of spring time. Funny how a light shade climbs my room. Where are you from, Mr Dragon fly. Very consider of course. Has to have come from Millionaires, name from laundry luck. Knows when business acumen steps into salvage. Friendship bask at shipping men. Beard at back door greet consider graces. Wild pitch relinquish short bread. He went for Ruth, like a long lost store card. He will have gone there when we were away. Something in the carpet told me of his treading. Crumbling passage of approach now, familiar from when he stood by the tops. Two pints daily skewered by black birds until cream became a Marco Polo. Life buoy neighbour with mileage drinking down gulf streams to current ports of Cretian. Lackadaisical creation. WAKE Up go-go ye spindler with coffer cuff links. Security measure Victoria. Vivian traces cups of tea for the brewery. Stolen child (1) Stolen child (2) Stolen child (3) Stolen child (4) Life is care free. Bicycle chain a kind of clip. Nonny clip clop. Tuning fork reason. Coast by on a wagon wheel. There it is, right in front of you if the logic isn't solved soon! Whole noise will erupt and just imagine all the lava there was in Pompeii. All the granite in Aberdeen and all the mountains there are to climb in Scotland. Tuning fork of thunder bolt. Bay through consultancy. Why dark reach for commune. Aladdin's treasure and tin charmers rub away for any potion. Reach infinite choirs of appeal to drown dumbing side effects. So many stigmas in so many lay bys, suggestions visited. Dusk of dawn of duck. Splendid in robes and concrete stools to constipate antagonism. Wreak war with fire lighters. Stoop crackle old stob against the swinging of talking gates. Spool drip with gunge, cheese and almond. Donut pave Dave's slab. dentist cheer in outrage. Tankard next day. delivery fact, etre, be he. Memory consult clause. Not that is sharing my delivery. These yours are my sees. Cake from a quality Street Tin. Purple sweet not mine in given. Change gone hand to address, pick your own raspberries. Verbal with peeving related horrors. Not much more than will. Crocodile clip lab stools, disposal with selection Wednesday. Bin man has been. Channel news fetched day to day last year. Now they wait outside. Sizable pip translucent in ebb. Stirring bowl contain pip stop dop dash draw cab taxi rank. Next spoon in boil. Courgette quote spelling carrot dices. Soften sides of christmas past the ear drum. hoove and hear in squeaky clean. Swallow capillary as a simile. Dr Peter Carey on the lobe as customer rating. Tune of nutrition uproot harvest troops. Labour with soil tend violet stand. flowering two weeks, nothing more. Bind independence of the week, and never seed inside a table. Rubbish on country lanes is a freedom. footpath small smile. Girl in blue dress by splodgy worm in Essex. City a god store with harmonised food packs and resurfaced efficiency. No harm in two rise conundrum. Your memory lies with me after the war. Sand and sea your mum is walls and peers. Holiday on a moped with marbles and some friend who is climbing trees. Beach towel with slate and chalk, Greek Fetter and pickles in York. Coast breathing toast and teething. Yakult and vitamin D. Feng shui that lighted candles. Memory astray lit the living room. Country fell a walk, with wetness and rain stumble and strain, order collect pebbles and feathers as emblems of treasure.

Memory line a far off place where languages lived. Crucible to hiding place. Your memory is mine. Your memory is time sat with two brothers. Wet hair and tide adrift on the crying moon. Rail collection goad laughing trance of uniform. Memory is actually agog, memory M is memory G. Celery in loss, difference albatross. Hid Radion program. Claimed foundation with footstool legitimate. Kicked in thick clause bucket. garnet Hijack of Green grasses. Wyoming trilogy, My friend Flicka, Thunderhead, The Little White Horse, The Enchanted Wood. Hyphen arrival through Bank of England view of Bangkok. Sudanese sultan, Maharajah of Bognor Regis, Daily news and bag of Sherbet dip. Bank of Norway, Bank of Sweden, band of Wales, Bank of Papua New Guinea in last stakes at Wentworth. Shimmery shiny bank of hotch potch, Lebanese freight train, Californian governess for Canadian geese. Stray new insurgence of key tone. Fourth

Musketeer. CC Dish of the Day in Mayfair. Next person catch
taxi wife. Lifeboat manager. Typist halve the cast of Scottish
dancing. Frigate of indulgence. Protestor fresh haggis. Book
keeping staples, Mrs Oliphants left shoe and The nuclear DinN.
Party written before about topic cases in sturdy columns.
Indifferent to papier mache
a1 b2 c3 d4 e5 f6 g7 h8 i9 j10 k11 l12 m13 n14 o15 p16 q17 r18 s19
t20 u21 v22 w23 x24 y25 z26
12 if the number isn't, then b2 goes nicely as 1b or even 2b in
order to get of a.o.b and all the gloom of Hamlet. Confucius
follow a program of better living rooms. At least with a
greenhouse car and rhododendron citric. Establishment blame
road network. Probably just another hose for playing digger.
Roaring road works digging people to rush hour traffic far
in the country. Wota climate lays down the wires and strims
epilogue fugues in c minor. envy trod the trace of buried
treasure. Beneath path in cables and growth pattern. Sewage 17
assuage. Le weekend, 57, e313g, Lock head on, sim, earn, head
sponge courtesy of cadbury courtesy. On holiday in animal
farm. Cat say dog say mouse say house. Never let a saucepan
boil dry. Open the end first. House says Simon in case it didn't
guess. Art in heaven hallowed kingdom come be done on earth
heaven forgive. Trespass forgive trespass. Deliver temptation
from evil. Kingdom power and glory, deer exception. Part time
bramble speculate for satellite, even tho t'was feared those
outside would not reach wellness. Custom fed bribery animals.
Caps are manicured too. Parable stamp proof en provence.
Buda tour guide, caravan smile, open. Bean posey. Safety catch
of history will not go down. It's On volcanic quarantine.

3

Berkoff wrote solitude into the lines of my brow. Consider reason left to treason. Folly in the course of a paragraph. Begin when banks were mountain passes, slipper construe raspberry ripple, deep pools of brown ochres to clap. Edge moor howl noises into patterns after commas. Render weekend of dressing gowns. Close to Hannibal forms of lecture. Pop and saliva all over the place. Weird thick forms of air in collision with Met office maps, card bard fuse xylophones, lentils and digestives, party spray, billboards and pop stars, expulsions, revulsions, Domesday and lesions. None are criminal. Take Ajax seriously. B side alphabet in rhyming steps. Just behind next banger and lexicon. Offspring jitter tap. Dynamo prescription tip old school clock. Pause mention digital energy. Broken light by Eros. Harpoon soft spy latch. General degree bodes soft kinesis of going lightly. Course of action cramp military curb. roaster gaze to odyssey with falsey lashes and wonder.

Try on the residence; line of address. Fulcrum designate bleeding, one full stop. Add it before Soho. Detriment jolly parson sit by perfume store with a blocked nose. Bank range of literary curses. Creep dam and rail seclusion inc. Relay margin crazy store, distance no object. Excited meteors. Light house partition as waves charge deflection. Second anachronism. Tear flood back ache. Inward bathroom like mobile phone. Striven edge in contract completion. Girl nig nog carton, felling with high yield ratios for dinner. Sad agent. Four eyes as if the supermarket hadn't done a bar code. Well really wot is going on round here. Anything worth asking. Wee bairns wi funny new place. Forage playful shape. Cousin box potato. Scones of spider plants. Courage throw sanctuary Cord. Root by hand establish miser. Confer home in stealth by emulation. Pop art catchment scuff grit. Elm's bough. Plasticine press squid. Meniscus on particles. Pendulum cone hard shoulder. Curfew turn guard wheel. Furtive picture cover shop setting. Bread mountain spend Friday. Lunch scrape soft blend. Love dog bow wow marvelous. Brian semi detached, fairer with company. Ozone laugh comparatively, blowing sneeze liquid on similar drains from Liverpool's smock. Explain without brochure. Tyre proposing quaich. Rubicorn oar fellow fable. Slice mitigate adventure. Tutor gate with supermarket options. Not necessarily cheap in sorrow. Impair forge canon. Barge in pool division. Vintage transport in whoever likes turkey. Perform about Constantinople. Canvass further among clipped pigeons. White feather gin palisade. Defeat low gear. Brisk wind invade blue water and inflation. Caution excitement drive zoo. Toll bridge of ice cream until pink rose. Twenty years later planted a while ago, possibly papered over. Lists of events. Episodic sequential, boils believed. Ram never came to much. Started in the waiting room. Hungry drips and mouth appearances. Milliner Kubrick smokey lens. Slither on laurels along with west ships and other tribulations. War and peace. Artifacts curdle on. May queue endure treatment. Begin with snare trader. It was never intended that a tennis Court should have spoken in tongues too. Draw a spade. Per 190 35.5 % same button RDA in vitamin D per 190g. 110.5 110% in vitamin B12. Stabilising whipping cream with dextrose, tetrasodium diphosphate sodium alginate wheat flour. Somebody stuck in the pipe, suck flush sugar. Vegetable oil strawberry jam 8% glucose strawberry sugar syrup acidity regulator punctuation please citric acid sodium citrate colour anthyamins gelling agent pectin butter. Water glucose soya flour milk chocolate sugar cocoa solids milk solids whey powder emulsifier soya lecithin flavouring muectant sorbitol salt fat reduced cocoa powder emulsifiers mono diglycerides fatty acids colour beta carotene acidity regulator citric acid flour treatment agent. Produced in the UK Stamford St London SE1 9LL.

Tiffany grow investment with chortles of telephone time. Same way Mildred grew conversational hair over beat of Heathcliff's hooves. Moorland strait under preservation from lens of magnified seclusion. Gallery myopic omnipresence as jugular biscuit interface, and the Carmichaels are not invited. Davy returns windowsill with broad brow of secret scrutiny. Private lounge and prescription rule consequence, mantle of moor a sacred workshop. Night ramble gather cones, PA replace toner. Song time insult and enhance Swiss bouillon for all semesters.

Menu

¾¾¾¾¾¾¼ = Guest speaker

Q.A. NOYES.

As a matter of fact, chewing on lines, Juliet lamb in a new consideration. Pavement of any pretensions. Slow and unreasonable leads to corners, strait produce were it not for the impression. Everyday Avery labour give away. Country living kick after five hour drive past Surrey sequences, beachey headland crown brow. Southern cliff top as if sheep should love. Mavis grown to love gloom of youth with a renewed zeal of posture accountancy. Life pass on turn styles of infliction that steal envy so she need not guard against it. I've never met Mavis. Came to me suitably tailored for friendship in small hours of embarkation. Decide interest aboard destiny for safety reasons. Booze and fags past flirt junction, meddling honour of curfew and grace, strive distance between man and dust bin liner. Lineage of Cilla stretch plain birth mark, wart into working frigidaire. Tonic and gym blast passage nuance with migratory rhythms of DIsCO. Big voice blend outcast in habitual mercy for lost causes, endangered species and neanderthal tides of rectitude. Real deal rare. Language of custom precede suitable onion like furlongs of layered shells that dim the washing spin. Lust incarnate beckon Graham and showdown commence. Enthrall Alan Partridge Chapter. Glow the catch without a cradle. Garden of azaleas, cat full of cotton wool. Lantern kitchen curtain with fish for blurry slurry mingles, fresh drawers. Cat created growing up cat. Teddy keep lavender. Haberdasher wild cat. Tom cat on stage. Macavity digestive biscuit, birthday seat condense nestle cans of cherries for crunching. Margarine line slabs as bricks upon which the cat stalks. Lest we stray towards the Cromwell parlour with more Thunder Birds and wild budgerigars on collars like flying cats who don't believe fish fly. Din hot n cool with glove dye flux rising. Same page walk paper man and prophet. Air mask of book long folded in camouflage of love. Four sounds evening, singular blades, grass weave another boss of Oxfam. Wore Chemistry skirts and Damart in the League of voluntary will not sway. Buckle draft exclude the name of persevering winds. Long socks and garters hand out poppies showing difference. She was met through surveillance of pink wafers and drop scones, ivy shadow of curtain leaves close to path of flapper box. So much in the end that it really did arrive. Hovercraft swept up outskirts of common sense. Struck tooth and nail of aging stys on duty. Boss gather pastry as jettisoned flour unsifted, golden smash core of mile by measure. Basket weaving signifies rehab. Second after plains of Australian labour. Paris Retreat after office paid in kind. Specific GAP of youthful intermission in whirls of opinion. Third persons of reaction. Attention parrot under belt of stature in mourning. Neon plasterboard above Davy's desk collected. Units of yellow biro notes and felt reminders complete occupation of clutter. Unhappy days subscribe underlay to recent plans. Obscure a real agenda of municipal life. I've never met Davy. Spotted a rinse of him across the television. Courgette of a prize vegetable. Davy will come to encounter seven episodes in a large principle. Brutus an absolute Fortune's cookie. Hair longer, why the hocus pokus. Dog bark sullied means on dreams. Swell course finger.

Type toe tapper with high heeled rapper on big hill. Look at it this way. Side angled lens of caution, single brain jostle for comfort. Heal a line that falls for paragraph. We're going into retail.

Murder 1. Fable on the table slowly.

Death 2. To old car and linoleum.

Bailiff trails past the store room. Folly skip that this will all be written down. Pence high wired fence. Leather belt a blether. Alison there. Looking glass over her shoulder. Large dog blew chain away. Single facade stepped on toe and winced with laughter. Poor you, she though out loud before onion ripe goat salveson that we deny sorbet. Mango dalliance means that you are frozen. Life crystal collect on ochre ledge. Tide call out to white head. Small grain the parting centrally, fetta coagulent with zest and speculative winsake. Draft cultured portion where demonstration stands. Matron path fine ardour. Left left stop space. Stop left alone. 12345 mounting right up space, famous last words. Count house counts. My count and whether or not we are able un due x. Troy rate of exchange, knee keep a cap on things. Silk ribbon tie pressure cooker. Quite raspberry ripple chocolate banana black currant. Delilah where's your wall chart. Block of brick take reason for the entire world together with exact proportion of science and half of persuasion. If you succeed in plotting left hand in front. Epicenter horizontal herpes going from. Wisdom gold with space for old boot. Chance for blubber concede frames with florida crust. Whence sincere lady grow own wings of division. Siphon mortal wear from culinary Carex. Get gang remain, cause for millennium. Tiger hollow cream of pancake. Ready again face edge of bowl, drip moisture profits from plate. Oven designed for globules. Mist sauna crackling strawberry ones. Ravenous porch sweep brightly to yield adjusted nostrils. Odour underarm gunfire. Harvest justice bed pen, mattress of bygone refreshment. Topiary doll in breadbasket on show. Sappy fool excavate bookshelf. Middle perfume not fit for

Marie Claire. Potpourri fine with leisured admiration. Abstain drags of manipulation. Clear afternoon of dizzy junket from party pooper. Please sit quietly without spamming forward checkout. Forty minute lapse. Inhibit fallen studies where lunch castrates queue to inches. Good morning Windolene, won't you sit quietly on your granny's triumph of being here for mother's school run. Brain inhabit those ears so like yer uncle Jimmies, monstrous. Tact separate features of collections. Bring in all sorts of from reports. Who intrude position of address.

Language carry on talking. Literate mingle dogs bodies. Music like a load of cods wallop. Play fast process. Station day deft. Stethoscope lens for healing. Single burned into the dyes of secular cohesion at least until die hards of special objects. Practice slumber an active presidency. In the meantime there are some people without hobbies who sit around in preview for best agenda. Tremendous in minor projects. Cycle to work have mortgages. Raise up dead talent to see if it works or not. Appreciate favour for a double chocolate dropping. Informal interview preferable to the weird psychosis of blind fold pop star. Anyway why are they paid. Decent insanity a mild preserve of bad taste pretending to be indifferent. Market a backdrop without parents. Anything to do with germination . Rely on a handful of people recently greasy. Endeavour whole heartedly unapparent. Tradition of sitting on pavement. Gutter until the end of. Degrees issued with millicent forecasts. Entitlement or not. Twenty one years of ice cream. Meeting twenty minutes Greenwich meantime. Young brother more promising future than the rest of the tribe. No ideas of what is going to happen. Can't all be green.   Opportunity scale chart of nature. Combustive force led fields of chemistry. Pie chart on itching ambition grade street in elocution. For the most part, program Tony Slattery. Brain tumor don't dislike. Three layers of efficiency bord last lane judgement. Bad mile of road works hedge interface for municipal congregations. Letter permission submission. Quotidian exclusion. Format ABC for D. Last bramble row, if there is such a place on the train line with silly goodness on the shore of hammering little ping pang which means accuracy at all times and not minding if the next word is the right letter. Space with little little. Word higher than the other bit with computer. Spoken of tip tap. Qwerty age in back space. Persist as the first founder. Fortune end all blame. Insurrection shadow perturb. Protect feast on Michel Caine. Brains of slurry juices. Gorse on the flank of hiding. Growth in flurried expression. Singer engine blend and leer for pitch tongue. Bilberry without curse. Paranormal paranoia. Feint hop a meter. First wife blame charges. Brochure tarry onwards. Formation cumbersome in ridiculous plays of being paid losses. Spurs are pipes to the tune of supply. Fruition come of yellow oranges. Line in overlap. Moderation of the board of supervision. Without any hurry at all, heartbreak buttons up. Cardy caption stills the phrase. Colloquial breeze of you. After the flight of their decisions it is realised without passions of influence. No hostage settle the goods of duress. Sit breeding knowledge of soliloquy. And in any case the two tier system of obligation hides a tree man in level branches. Negotiation is calm on the tongue. Nonsense that some people spend on forwarding their past into some kind of trance. Belindering Cinderellas without normal coaches. Lids of lash mascaras. For who cares if the opinion is not gut welding to terms of as it happens. Presiding judge of Jellaba summoned the entire verse and psalm to a point that has language. Always trumps to understanding force of grounding. Square hole of small d turning. Some things don't change on centenary. Seemed that reminiscence lasts until Kings Cross. They all said polity g'bye and resumed measured intervals. World of a prefect. Carriage of the Edinburgh breed in causal relations. Stage for the loafer to comb in a display of swallowing sandwiches. Full of mineral essence. Outpost glaze trainer in casual wear for airs of sensitivity. Aren't that special, compatriots until Barbados. Begets the better of them fall privy to despotic bitterness in an age of anonymous celebrity. One of the girls could have been a car. Gleneagles influx of reeling. Thirty one White House Interns. Frame prospect per head. Overtake socks and sandal in legitimacy conquest, the way that car keys have. Time for nine, informative trip. Graft on last years performance, shoot lodge slant of inquisitive industry as far as a Russian connexion decided. Reconsider in taking aim to the skies. Jungle Formula helpful in establishing ominous as a scourge of mozzies. Planted bites for Dracula. Kind of the car to remind. Parallel consideration of bed eyed monster marksman, all in the blood. Centuries of tapestry stage atmospheric gentry. Rally cast out a mad infidel. If only it hadn't been me. Itchy marathon upon. Ghoulish presence run as a silly story. Starts from the gates of hell. Well trodden habit sustain innovation of new histories, specters themselves. Home, guard face and fortune, now and then. Illusion visual span tenses. Juggle tend the minder of being particularly aware. Which way leading themselves. If example must be insisted upon, birthrights of wild horses need to be imagined in this field. Enclosure incidentally. Choir sing Balthazar for seasonal rhetoric hum outside. Advertise the feeling of shoulder to shoulder. Sunday to skim through with pictures. Lately its been a telegraph whose sense has been tempered by weekly style. Shed the film of information. Equal stars on CCTV. A William camp have come up with features on freshers, promise of complexion. Braves displays of example by precedence. Stride alternate heritage and jeans. Savour the odds of two parents. International progress is good. Benches are not at war with the cloakroom. The IRA look like pretty fools. Compulsion determine undermined, TV turn friendly. Train delay by sixty minutes to allow settlement. Perth platform near array of pot plants.

So I lounge with an outstretched elbow on luggage. Deep sunshine pack appreciation. Whirr gently over the railway bridge, driver share a measure of access. Sweet cost in confection that never crashes. Northern lines of industry. Continental sweat fuels the notice of export by chimneys and land scars. Holiday failure gobble at success. Construction flights on seas of environment. Replace sign with plaque. Bonnie exfoliate savage for cool income. Came to visit mind sweeping. News chips for everyone who hadn't found Italian, free parking, nurses, farmers and lawyers. Darwinian remote control of staple contingency to the human form. When yer livin with an ape, everyone's a dog collar. Most interesting holiday bargain, deemed that Charon had lost control of his job. The way that people speak to each other through the fanny of a six year old is a strange design for a mouthpiece. Camp in the woods get back to nature beyond personal description. Prune roses meaning to. Coincidence has been marking time instead of listing it. Method generally melodrama in cerebral halls of capacity. Artist response permissive at most borders of lenience, though taking action less possible. Kidnap backing out of the driveway. Wonder at the coarseness of solid stone, how trellised force of three large steps should still bear the weight of the gorge. Clarity shaft light through gushing water. Imminence of place a forest floor. Juxta pose any hidden treasure. Barbecue of mown grass perpetuate myth of splitting time in two and of tripping down hopscotch for a glimpse of tomb stone boulders. Hedge a stone stairway cave, bridges and picnics. I've been here before said the pudding to the starter although in those were times. Follows me through is the hued voice of worn slippers, fast trace of the circus, tangly styles of hair, cummerbunds, long slugs in the rain, fame, caterpillars, uncollected rubbish and H2O. Too late to go calling on the gate, so I trod on by an assurance of keeping appointment. Echo in the state of remembered faces met. Kitchen lunge and the podium are all vocabulary to this mountain pass. Sequel cause the quarry of hiding diamonds. Betray to the cats eye. Circumstance of encouraging weather and crunching chestnuts, chapter nestles against the visiting islands. No matter what the adventure of Enid, this returns when the tall slope gives way to a new goodbye. I have not been recovered. Tall trees of oaken branches because of rest in their decorum. Boum party through souls of jolly singers, look on the legal wrangle which trades conformation. Deportment with ignorance. Barn of the owl, tasty frame of mind removed like a slide rack of changing slides without commentary. Forgive sentiment of tangibility, witness a stop. I remember the mambo in little black Sambo. Inevitable course of striking notes as letters from arithmetic. Reconvey an old friend. Attempt when theory is not a written quotation. Bargain larger rations of time, knowledge beyond the syllabus of hearing. Things are static now. Where are the gypsies, vagabonds, the where do you want to be, small fledgling, simple story mother place. Where is your wind span, elephant caravan. All sucked up by Daddy long legs. Signs chumping from inversion. Coercion go on, give it a go then, do the actions. And so she did the actions and this is what she sung. Praying hands, tilted head. Same and then the other side. Obvious with lips I dreamt. Hands out, just funny lady with green fingernails. Recollection grafting and a layer of emotion. Event stone the moor for a hill pony. Best friend for a place on the shadow of instant'. Order come to perfect the innocent course of guilty. Badge way in Mercedes, thrall as a passenger for ten years. University post reunion, as if a crisp scored a goal. Other bidding bewilder the Afghan. Forgiving introduction in supposed to achieve. Stroke a whisker in grooming. Appall size of development so that forlorn greed mourns fantastic promise. Berate a weasel in the youth, save that homage dwindle. Different kind of lance. Bow of weather over the hair line and cheek the aid of understanding. Wise crack of Bryony, not that I've read the book. Passage stumps of beauty, weird cloud of ecstasy enhance sharp object. Induce to un lynch mobs of conduct. Il y a un. Olders and betters plagued for free dinners. Better tow than wrong master. Unity hilt of incandescence, what does that mean. Summon populates to remind the brain about Asian reaction. Disdain for the confused line of friendly suitors. Event glare the smile, interval and commentary. Connect Four is where I'm at. Such an old typewriter since the symbol. Serenade neighbourly on a dear white gate. Providence next door patch. Obligatory old food is tasteless and without degree. Reappraisal isn't automatic tenure. Down turn weren't as they seemed of mother bounteous, letting things slide. Wake cruise on from shore landing. Pet the guise of gallantry. Mission of sailor suit circumstances, loyal battalion to the cost of satellites, miniature sagas and the great unfolding. Planes can fly oceans into clear view for the sake of not pointing a finger. Complexity witnessing horror not about two hotels for the price of one. Virilities are shaven. Forgiveness never owed credence in return. Completion when oversight appears to have skipped the booking exchange. Line of trees kept a hive of bees. Clouds have been floating for some time across the plains of Britain, and since the derision of sky larks is a show unnoticed, man chooses to settle in the style that suits him. Convict a careless loss of memory so that imposition mark in manner of all men. Most things appreciate the curve of learning, curls a neon glow in writing. Mock scribe subscription, pleasure curse of righteousness. Semi colon end of paragraph, thank U2 good evening. Enhance further trees and Amazonians. Multiple twangs of delirium, full bodied and illiterate, depletion plays round the corner. Seljuk enter Viking hedgerow of suburban deer. Invite permission un cajoled. Clear pontefract archipelago. Grain dapple check. Toby spot for dancing by instruction. Modular disciplines won't flash, subtle brand roll sanctions of dispersion. Ensure a different number of good sweets. Fraction adjust cogency metered in perpendiculars. Flap with vibration. Grab cylinder off to the park, lever kick the ounces. Clop a blackbird on the ear. Leverage bend tiller out of season. Notes on man with bangles and rabbits but man from poster well presented stray. Arm says write that gel spheres from sheaths. Entrance first act of significance. Penalty serve love's investiture standing base prides with electricity to blind alley fieldings. Affection plainly states in single lines. Challenge by lip sentry peals of laughter. Session colonnade resume plinth amendment by draughts on leaden pan. Apostrophe NYC in speech that lend erroneously for the fun of juggling. Non oppositional burglar mediate subjective replacement. Bookish rentals enrich foul play haunts with valour. Knock knees on sticks chisel bark 'n growl fences Marjorie swaps feet the barracks, impeded by choice. Chance marries the fold and familiar. Trod claims heel mountain. Kingdom Robbie began with a lesson of instructive persuasion. Paper trail start with indication to go, note to read, no hair to consult, and no quest save the Holy Grail. As with states of confusion, reason obliges conference with impartiality, often in the form of a riddle. November on turnstyle, live stock barn. Grand union of June. October place, park trace. Avenue bicycle has sheep in hiding. Original flora bay leaves. This is not Demetrius. Difficult autobiographic work of personality has arguable tedium. In many ways this is the object. Single currency story telling a clean up job of assimilation. Propriety and flare mask bald removal vans and side cars. Facility of YOU is valuable. Understudy cloaking daggers. Enquiry legend unfold as an Oxford companion. Persistence deserve you. Mind panel on TV, busy body firing silent from rebuffs of photon caption. Balinese horse in context of heroism. Know side of box. Pandora rod nap. Schedule inversion busy with news reviews of Shipman Saviour. Lady cape on changing lifeboat mind. Shore sign of emigration. BBC7 takes a full half hour. Weather included along with Jeremy Paxman. Wogan's abominable car wash. Friday music room with Gabriel's arms bands. Host for signing 'n'. Chat show convey manic message of incubations. Murmur trigger of cheesy spotted birthday pies. Message every pop song. Harold on Tuesday, with all that hair but for what. Saw a friend on Thursday, for it turns out Sebastian really is a snail. Goldilox is one of them. Those are my companions, more than evolution and the MRLP. May they always lie in capitals. I'm reading this out in a speech. Third person enter third person. Funny lady number four. Fourth person enter fourth person. Funny invitation through the letter box. Funny lady will have to go to it. Nothing more astonishing than a stamped addressed envelope with an edict. Related on time. Greenwich, Los Angeles, Rio, Singapore, Delhi. Cat essence equations. Confiscation of royal mail, ever consigned. Gizmo pulling faces. Envelope resign in flap top lap of Burgundian triptychs. Zip sided cow calf on loan for birthdays. Present his worship for introspection so outlook may be Debretted.

Bibliography track Roxanne. Track root track drum kit. Track Yehudi track fading out track birdie track My Girl. Muppet track god save the queen track mercury track olly hackers has got nothing to dotwith George Harrison's piano. Where kiss track the surgery. track not that they were to know. Track cat Moulin marine track Yasser was not the plastic population. Track Banarama track much better take off track is-there-anybody plastic that isn't included with barbie track bubbles. Track feed the world track scaffolding track snowman. Track it should've bin me track velvet underground track sight and sound. Track and l track Chaplin bedcovers track Diana track Joseph in the stable track staple track remote control track visiting track track returning track friend for life track seal track dolby. Track grey owl track dead or alice track question track siren track administering track who the fuck put me on so many drugs track hello track baby snatching track in her long grey coat track wayne track decibels track the yew tree track over the border track looking to me track reference track Audrey track new line. Track Christmas track Kiki saw track the pink house track paris track the large dark cloud track let there be light track another escape track so many uses for a small pair of nail scissors track white water rafting track the staler track protection tract the infiltrator mark Healy track my ear track next phase track overwritten track seal again track the Ethiopian. Track the very large pacific ocean track survival track the Orient express track those huge waves and such a mal tiny blob and all that way in the cruel sea track nobel prize track psychiatrist chair track the mercy of the beautiful water track hostage in the neighbours garden track Rothschild. Track Jolly Roger track the next day is next track weeping market places. Track do we have to put in the polpot pinochet world leader conference. Track leukemia track radiotherapy track yes track video track optical illusion. Track turkish delight track don't like it anyway. Track brain scan track treatment track bills bursar y track cheque plus account track test track medical track mental track test LP track CD track test leaves on the line track Bulgaria track not enough notes on the line. Track trains track teeth track yank them all out. Track plastic surgery track look at my cheeks track spotty lip track sticking greta pins and needles track bog down her laboratory track her in his track the amalgamation of treason. track nine nine nine to be continued. Missed out on TOTP trac one to forty from there to then and now again. Immediate ageing a short flight in fancy. Where on earth did the eel come from. slapstick Those teenagers are genuine company, shedding through tides of location. plow the potter, gardening. small boy play the violin. Attic the prefect handwriting. whisky afternoon, Irish gnome, decadent nicer geography. maintenance fixtures are in trouble. We meet the Blue Planet of Island Indigents at a firework display of tooth decay, all smiling. piles of seated composure. Eclipse neanderthal drum beats of outcast warehouse. Bus shelter and homing device. Used since the capture of Troy before car parks or international. After before progress. Breathing fill stop. Take a vision of white shroud and street lamp. Florence not the nightingale. Bird song of a dying day. Peat and whisky plowed the field full cycle and pattern shies onwards without fashion. Waist navigation. Wednesday's play was good. Arabian palaces sat next to her flatmate, and then the thin stick who painted the tiles and who didn't relate so well to the flat one because of her name. Must be more reasons to Luther as the beginning of women's lib. Organisation of space realised careers of key lime flan which will hopefully keeps condensed. Freshness for Tuesday's event. Receiving will renovate progress, depending on who can come. Dinner check up closeness, and I still only wish for an online friendship than I have ever really had. Mutual sense is an old sister. Many washers, not exclusive right of way. Guides the motorists. For those on bicycles, checking into a sports shop is a hazard, considering water supply. Escape exhaust. Where is my voice fixture. Tie dye far from this old man with a nick knack. Beauty clinic as Eiffel Tower of liposuction, triumph in suspension and other processes which don't equate in the same way as forms of compliment. Anecdotes of calm for hurdy gurdy insolence. Nemesis of stratum, acquiescence of penultimate income, obstruction of destiny and they all depend on doubtful word search. Sit across the wheels of random push chairs formulating debate as if it was valued by license. Indeed, my lords and ladies must be toffs of pattering hearts, must be wise ones. Tree top toffs and healthy past time boffs, thinking toffs on buses from here to Peterloo. Toffs of all costs in the galvanising throng of wandering sequence and toffs to stay on after the party. There must be. Confusion of toffee knowledge needs to be claretfied and whiskied into vintage masters and splintage on brain springs. Give in to the master card. Cross eye teeth ripe with dentistry. Squawky infra dig sets to daily rumble. Parachute for the safety strap, as any dog wags. LG is three in one. Life as a highland breed has led to the low ground. Order take stock to shooting stars. Anarchy through a tally for blame. Save the abscess capsule. Theseus, brave slave from Pythagoras, when he was writing a thank you letter to the Great Dane of Glamour this side of the Tigris. Thessalonica five months later than prophecy, when music is much better. Life in the pond is prone to algal bloom and rare species of gurgle on the desk top. Discovery quite a lot to report from the ice berg, count Mondays in queueing bricks, Tuesdays in thinking. Wednesday's of monsoons and brothers of long and lanky. Treasure blurb dictation. Further heaven brought boxes in bodies of dead enlightenment. Engine room afloat when deposition took stake in practice. Valuable like skin cream and yoghurt, sweet straw reminding Simpson and Delilah. English was a great episode of M and W. All the more interesting for an after dinner spiel on forestry. Simple Ireland a merry banjo. Tippy within reach, according to surface area. Wall colour plans without being too suspicious or anything. Providing the network supplements the chocolate freize in little men on stair cases. Get in touch with collection, short presents shouldn't trouble, providing there isn't an enquiry on insinuation within breakfast. Wind up as if the situation should be provided within the scope of gardening fractures. Patron tone will ever vacate the apple oesophagus. Besides Brixton, any wonder that insides are overtaking sense which leaves trains open to digestive prize giving. We are not shedding humour on the preposition of five year plans. Mere manipulation, but fortune will prevail. Silesia separatist commented their own design that new style Persil was not necessarily a compliment. Put it down to next door. To do with the voice over. Walking prospect has nothing to do with diocese scales or autocue. Really ochre meal. Underside of ship. Whole Albert injunction, who don't think much of it. Nerd three and all for a big poetry motion. Stupid blur and skinny man worried about croon luminosity. Concerned with getting to the bottom of things. Made sweat for a while but effusion lasted, and took intertwined over many other conspirator. Israeli just for the evening. Mind the runway of puffing exotica trips. Personify a bull fight. Justify margins of past pensions, chew nibbles past sausages and peanuts. Perhaps market forces keep separate hours of distinction, how artful. S o n s o r l o v e r s heart attack condition. Sway to conclusion. would it remain just alive, beat overcome short pages. Remember feeling sorry for art. Bought the brown Dylon. Confession of trivial implication. Mad onions, everything plural and indiscreet, bay city roll for a handful of chives. Chest of worry protect a plastic lining. Wander into market cavities of crisp stocking shop. Strolls passing clouds. Ingratiate has taken block busting out of its sails, he is my relief tho some fool could carpet bag a letter head of basic circumstance. Slug mention pop and there ye have Burkina Faso. Good slug thinks he's a gardener. Route recorded in projected slime. Construe this maths to have one leg shorter, measure in the gallery antennae. Indy pop. Curfew raw consumption sing a mangel of Aquarius Esterhazy. Depress phases of sugar. Enough to detract bags of pop corn form the city junction. This afternoon friends in comfy jumpers. Still can't leave the media alone. Crunch past is an evolutionary soap. Living recorded giving and taking. Much more preferable than the pre Columbian wasteland of not having a hat or wearing wrong pajamas, grieving into the wind, answering questions as if it was doctrine, remembering navy blue as a matter of bread and butter, watching changes during lunch. So much depended on what was going to happen after lunch that I became as grateful for the chicken running on a battery energy. Game corn where every sideways is of suiting plain things. One week later and I ask you to consider the astronomy. Yearn symbols of indomitable wealth which guard acres of shrouded stealth. Unborn streams of incubating farts from diagonal of weather arriving on bicycle seas. Host the olympic nest of all picnics. Western Germany so please tend with pride and salami and pay due needs and requirements of such a naval officer, given that he has now landed with planetary arms. Field of prognosis from whence no surrender with faith and no victory with flag. Given that certain belongings are quintessentially cellular, it is not intended that he should leave, untouch tooth paste flavours should be an inherent clause. Pastures that fledgling tracks of maintenance should incur a space between fixture. Cover front owe Britannica expertise, human and back street forecast. Miscellaneous fling. Should the interred presume permission to disrupt discourse. Ritalin, opium, bad smells and soda water can be washed down with Mary's dairy, non clotted. Lord Tycoon has a straight jacket record in baby cord. Classification animal mineral well done marsupial mamal bird fish. Amboeba liquid gas in the sauce of learning. All said sooner happened to the scribe. Bogey man, fortune day time TV passer. Sprouts fifty times four hundred leaves bulbs. Serve with home made jam, can be mouth watering. Sun up for action. Paint the end of sunlight far away in Wales and take a head stand to MBNA. Molar do my excercises. Nutcracker large for a door. Somehow have a diary. Worry a cam corder. Outlive somebody to rest in deep water. Cliff seascape without plateaux in rockery. Stay alive could cost an album. Incarcerate anemone need feed like the sacrifice of Helgar to Davy wheatcrop. Shovel mix aggregate to pave over mud and undesirable damage to footwear. Churn with fabular chemistry that everybody knows about. Income from states of affairs which brought unprecedented closeness to the allies by frights of simple spiders. Oh, Miss Muffet, there must be some other way to persuade you, said the large spatular of wriggling. What do worms do. Spear mint is unlawful. Wee ball bouncing hell yer sell boing boin bab boy-ing. So long Sammy Jo, Jim Bob Mary Ellen, Jimmy Sue. Employ the bogey man. Garden sparrows fled next appointment. Four am forty, six I am sixty. Conference about interims of ten years, but another ten have gone by until the printed word has approached ransom. Wining over with yule tide ain't much use in strategy, save the old sentiment for an arguable case. indiscriminated of the umbilical measure. House of Grey Hound that watches unwound grains of primary seconds. Discarding leaves for non renewal, yet why should love speak its name, for it is not invited in trial, and will not loom the weave unspoken. Repeat the hymn again, but in another loft conversion, in another enclosure, in another century with different toes and other breathing, with more variety. Give me more variety next call time elephone, give a bit of credence. Semi colon dwell with more sense than the charging bloom of buttercups posing as fat drops in soup for every day consumption. By the way, this was supposed to be entitled Cream Slice with the appendage. In order of appearance; Thin Wedge Filling, but not on this page. People have been catapulting with innuendo so its tempting to line them up from Murrayfield to the flint stone pellets of fast living cave men on a tea break from ostrich farming, not to mention the greats of double standards. As agencies go, talent or introductions salute Herbaceous borders of Garden schemes millennial in the queue for supplement bunkers with all mod cons and condiments, cata-baly-tonic for a score on laugh hysterical with complexity stooge through applicatory monogamy to randomly know the digit. Number to a work force. Sign on response capital R and Res ponce. Sure honey response. Radio give prize caller thirteen for being both unlucky and right about the phonetic sound of Co-Ca-Co la. Anarchy stewable that super trance beats alternate. Farm justice jets of international coagulate for a great topic. Encouragement needed adventure tale. Inventions are like collective dandruff with small voices of on both shoulders of the beaker. Does anyone want back slapping neglect. Blue bottled message is YO. Distrustful of supper and glasses but sill go without gloves or independence to stake out gooey fodders of explanation since raw seeded chance of Diaspora. Work shopping immunity so grapples the chore of investigative doorsteps. Elliot persuasion transmission is leave choice to gates with Rolling Stones. Lurk of late luck stall buck empty truck for wimps capital double you. Question sooner for McEwan is a cavalier beer. Margins get the TLS as a normal life placebo. Name poleaxed with euphoric combined with half terms of chocolate mouse pasta quills and seventy pound shopping for growing men and appetising stimulate. Wonder relaxing. Churn offset the big name, all for joining a plan of importance, objected to a spot on the windy wall of climbing roses. First address of record binned. Scot in murder sped. Some aren't for asking. Turner catch zipper. Plural opinion outside one's own mental circle. Quote supersed propriety of known mettle. One can rise in a dead language. Intones suppose garden for the sake for nourishment bled, forlorn, accused, misused, overrated, dispense gratis. Factory. Inevitable conquest between Saul and Gaul where x = x is bound to come up in conversation amongst those who make a habit of talking. Olympian foot rest carry motto daily. Corn where the rest have already been. Hunger should have caught up the ordeal of sledging a hammer. Curdled curmudgeon of hunk tear edgy chop of grilled breath. Slick vapour snip of green. Sheer passenger woken for batting again. The ball was in. Creak glaze hot chives. Session furl on tenancy leanings, chrome bills the motor bicycle. Terrible clan afoot. Tank drip tests then Gulliver runs in. Subject interfered there's not a gauge of terror, give it over, mind your own business travel card. Meditation publishes that a spade is a summary of multiple opinion. Permanent role play in doubt so speak snake role with custard. Single dream ever compressed as ironing. Blur in stereo lunchtime shy for gratitude. When the Falklands war was going on there were a million and one things to without probity. Chinese coup set Saigon. We were fortunate too. Olympians have a fine word for rules without war, it is necessary. Face another banner in slight wind, another flag of Julius, share a birthday rinse off brandy to render flush surprises. Face epilogue of substance, one with a father extra.

Blue nestle in boredom of masked reaction. Insist on intention pejoratively and similarly deserve relinquished in the hospital of enterprise. Black n blue n brown serve but head from thorax from abdomen. Condition in jumper trouser she cloth with hair as thread for missing skull. Divorce over occupation the way these follicles swim with jelly. Private interned to scout the next. Trainee has Hula Hoops battered and sauced by a shop corner. Wing sing threes brine.
In this manner the course of sentences had invariably wound along the veering tip of lullaby just as shoes would show had they the print of passage. Upward strait of diverse literature planted good stubs for the path of march fence. Decisive trances were feeding pigeons when they came to trans live good practice. Charlatan gooseberry winch mirror worry on reflective shoe stickers. More to this than shoes said the auto pilot in remote control thunder to the sparrow.
And when the dog awoke from the frightful spate of blinking toads. When toads thanked the blinking dogs for taking over, and when Avalon wrote the treaty of calligraphy in double line spacing to confuse down stairs from higher cares, it was legible to the wrong side of privet to appreciate jungular chaos.
Evening is a sheaf of paper, drawn out and destined for the scrap of common thoughts assembled. Neighbours live in close seclusion camping in separate lounges, adopted dreams shelved on hold for talking in plural episodes for trouble. Come to think of it Aids is an old friend, then the dancer, snail and long eared hare of Aesop in a collection of prose which marks out years in new releases, sessions and part conference times. Overhaul due to congregate upon ledges of infinite justice. Streams of rowing boats bask and slide through slippery coast of venture. There to be expected, paid for and relinquished. Learning as thermal flight in underwear. Shouting leaves the party in a terrible state. What happened as a manner of speaking. During dinner there had been a majesty of oatcakes on spread. Martha lent over backwards to prove it and found

cheese had been summoned especially. Found it difficult to hold a biro. Indeed, she held a pen to prove it. Never met Martha and neither have you. We shall now proceed with the main dish Davy Wheatcrop. Barley sugar advert tripped him over in the royalties clause. Sledging is over between slaves and reindeer. over the cloud of thunder carpets and mini hedges that guide the rule of overviews. Custom of frequent expedience. Howling gale march forth in isobars to relieve static junctions of infra strides. Left tethers, right weathers for girl in trollies and sightly binoculars. Creature shifts that drift long wood from briar tup and seagull. Hundreds of car parks from linoleum brackets and each ton initially cleaner. Christians came to name a conker. Chestnut ripens nuggets of brown warmth. Of all the statues in the garden, one that gives shelter from hail, tho it may be struck by lightning. lung of all minerals = shift + Conker cake, conkers, conquerers in conk west of birthdays knock. Fair eminent and counting. What are the rules. Davy Wheatcrop wakes up the office by dismantling the alarm. Chatter place tags call it a night and prepare for standby. Bagpuss purr murmuring lines. Interval no torture of conscience. Multi facet full stomach of man measured in density but weight of opiate or analogy. Personification course beyond scurvy disbanded. Green tea and lentil saturation of such effacing tones, trembling at leaves for correction. equation with reflection upon Davy. Plain sneeze bring wild soliloquy of mustard tension beneath shade of briars torn by moody tunes at dawn. Depend narcissi from council pot roadside. Stem awe plot gets read and put safe. Clover humble bee. Micron lofty thatch ahoy consider crossed leg. In case of having to hop home on a one man band wagon toppling blisters for pop stars and unusual dentures of everlasting baubles. Neighbour silent gesture slammed door inside pauper home signal milkman's orange juice with fizzy punch of UHT. Expectations all dominions encircling the fort against castle, ladders and stairs, whisks and arches benches and angles grown from root clippings. Uncle muncle dined with four stops of bitter in Cheshire. Less than surprised his conscience with a foreword. Common soap just phrases. Curricular pretend to understand. Wish it was gargoyle, not having to look multi dotted Ariel with a beam changer on horizontal guidance for their kind of forecast. Maybe there's a space for language and baggage, notes are interesting. Wobberley x y z wishes westerly wib in spite of everything. Conclusion Remove dearest exciting. Never mind goes writing Style. Sets an inspiration. Furniture with consummation. Have a seat in retreat. Talk aloud to defeat. Rattle off explanation. School ovation Constant answer. Equal question decimal. Measure Asian A to A at five point five. Doctor punctuation helpful. Bend what to think at night.

4
The Old Man

Tom would be the old man's name, abbreviated. Tom does chat shows on Sundays, he brings up fame. Tom is not Tom's name, he acts the classics that time understands. Modern day is Russian for all the pace, he could be retired. Tom has emerged from his large cave, just like a tortoise. There aren't many about, what practice there is to survive. Tom talks to the man with big ears on the morning, toot toot. Taste of coffee is planted in the foreground, society is sound. Tom feels personal issues re largely overlooked, trains mark sleepers to keep up with doing cognitives. In Tom's day factory sweat was honest and keen, boots were not deodorant. Tom appreciates the living clean are hard to delineate, simple inspectors. Tom is faced with technology, goodby ornithology. Tom is enchanted by harmless young applying art. Tom has been invited to an exhibition, he's the example. Tom is actually called Eon, everyone says hello Eon. Tom does handkerchief spat at the door, it was blenched in Africa, vogue to the prop room. Eon, not Tom says the lady welcoming. Tom is anyone's, they just have to reach grade. Misses bestowing welcome souls, lives in a chamber. Tom has played sorry reporter, seduced it. Who knows if Tom is a crashing failure. Tom isn't Eton. Equivalent were, needs of nowhere. Does have a television, can play cards. Tom may have seen E.T do the crossword. If Tom had chosen a more complicated eight year old dare. Tom's life is out of date, so there. In the old days, Tom would have blazed a path. Confucius of how to tie a scarf, that's a cravat, not that. Tom is a name, tabby cat purrs in coal man's home. Testicles discussed in Yorkshire and a gravy aunt to face. Corners left to cobblers with bent hammers. Tom has posture because of aunt, and doesn't deny her value. When Tom is important there is no holiday. Modern impression themes a moment, scruff for the cinema, stud break. Claustrophobia herds marriages to living agreement pension rates. Time to grow stale until retirement, earn money to keep busy. Russian time is not about homeland. The Old Man could have private devotions, may influence fatherlands for a rubber stamp. Tom aware of cornucopia but must remain agile with mistaken identity. Stories on Sundays flourish with costume development. Tom thinks eloquent and his lines are brilliantly terrible. Has to tap his foot at the barn dance. Weighs up old folks charter with back chairs in all the rooms. Old stare, young vague. Monotony is hidden in fluctuate fare, mark of depending. What time is the bus says Tom. Tom has been given a sitcom, two episodes. Tom isn't the godfather, it became the DJ's job. Tom isn't aware that he has a job, stands in for scenic. Even when there's a huge romance, Tom loops for emblematic blood on the hoof of speeding Miami. Boys under adolescence take time to talk to

Tom, he does have grand children. Tom coincides with mild habits and false perversity, Tom is the rare treat of Sunday's land, he cheeks a dimple. Tom's grand daughter likes the BFG and grows up looking back. Although she's in the story she can't appreciate it. Tom thinks actresses have too much to contend with, but they can rise above frustration. Masses of faults permeate Tom's palace in marble trophies. Tom can puff cigar and muse is bored by cronies. Cronies develop from frustration, this phrase can be misleading. Where is Tom going. problem dissolved for Tom, his grand daughter has been defined as Gorgonzola. Tom lives in an out of the way place called Lawrence of Arabia, he doesn't know Gorgonzola. Tom comes to know Gorgonzola by the political relevance she has with trouble.

Gorgonzola is a fruity cheese that would like to inherit a mansion. Gorgonzola lives in the ordinary canyon, she complains. Gorgonzola was earmarked in youth, rosetted by the Lust group of return performance. Gorgonzola knew that she was lusty and was set aside. Gorgonzola grows up on Gorgonzola, fed her own cheese. Admires who she isn't, thank goodness for that. Tom signals gentle clues as much as the old man can, Gorgonozola thrashes her weight with inference and pun. Lust group of return performance tease Gorgonzola where she goes, what a labyrinth. Gorgonzola fancies she is permutated, wants to know how she was created. Entertains the lust camp, becomes elected. Lust camp set up a membership called features for theatre. Gorgonzola required to lead an office life. Display defy the modesty. Has all she needs to excel in canapes and rosary beads. Fit society with brimming performance. top sledges of human technology needs no Scarlet O'Hara. precious doesn't advertise well. Gorgonzola is careless trapped in her own spell. Tom can't grasp leading lady immunology . It is felt that he would have access to ladies of swell. Hollywood has fountaineered to some extent, there are Elizabeth Taylor feelings. Sunny side understood has direct access to the screen, that's one pound fifty in nineteen eighty four. Great traditions of learned men keep together, watch Big Ben. perception of distinction in darning felt to be woman's rose. pace of come and go charges electric chairs. blond pass for brown when she dyes her hairs. Gorgonzola gets embroiled in social justification, does nothing but boast about iron casting. Gorgonzola says nothing, she grudges. Slot for Nicole Kidman Who could be like John the cowboy, Sunday afternoon's employ. Wild West full of interest and their horses canter more interest than William Hill's live bet. Resist Orwell is the job of a green bird on children's television. The green bird is called Orville understand. In many ways the potty trained are vulnerable, they take on tea leaf duty. Tom looks like Orville when he thinks. Rridiculous weighs upon meniscus. Ancient mariner explore beyond feature, frail to grasp fish. Constant renewal among business. The old man waits for spring, plan is juggling the brood to respect him. The old man makes three. The Old Man demands, fits his clothes or becomes concussed. When the funeral arrives the sky deals luck. High street rates of perm and pectin. The old man's gap was a tooth before. Tom has a complicated mind in character. Scrap personality gets away with lithe and jovial without even smiling. Focus of attention was never invention on what had already been made. Thrashed when he is on parade. What is his grand daughter doing. The old man's grand daughter is great and greater yet, there are five generations between her establishment. The old man has collectible glasses that he keeps for special occasions, reading knighthood in small print. The old man specifically likes Wensleydale cheese, so do Wallace and Gromit. The old man could recite a sonnet, do it justice with elephant skin. Wise about what he does and imparts to Gorgonzola with brushes. Philosophical about scraping a living, resorts to sandals and staying in from the rain. He had a vibrant life and then a pretender mispronounced the name of his wife. The old man has a rival neighbour that grows cress. Cress laughs at the old man, look at his chest! Old man's chest is Gorgonzola, if only she were. Cress fancies Gorgonzola, came from a barren boot that always caught Rubella. Cress is a pure seed that goes with salmonella, preparation of human dish is national program. Cress falls for lego to improve his astrology. Water feature of cleanest magnetism. Gorgonzola does her best to stay dirty. Afraid of being modulated perfection. Gorgonzola so disposed against being Egyptian. Mustn't wear eye liner. Disguises her charisma with frumpy nouns and slurred speech. Gorgonzola visits Cress one day, wants a typewriter to go his way. Why Gorgonzola should choose to waive is one of life's proclivities. Cress and Tom fought in the war. Deep drawer either side of the knee. Right and left handed Cress and he. Tom draws what he can from the light, Cress exposed to catch a sight. Tom has more reason. Autobiography, there's a public clamour. Irrelevant to the OAP. The point is that Cress is in the gay relationship with Tom's gorgonzola. Cress wasn't a proper scientist, just an efficient collector. Cress points out style, wanders with a sweater. Gorgonzola wanders in fashionable clothing, prefers jeans. Gorgonzola makes statements with coincidence. Nearest trolley in blowy weather. Grandfather of the sex slave rave. Tom is best at home. Cress is unreliably named, purest remarkable. Tom is heavily engraved and only a satchel. Learning fritters. Cress as a lost cause, can be salient. Cress implements Tom as ingredient. Tom fathered strays by losing pungent. Gorgonzola mothers a brand new wave of personal crave. Gorgonzola doesn't look like Tom, acts like Cress. Gorgonzola trips along, doesn't wear a vest. Gorgonzola enjoys being tussled, unwittingly related scores. Gorgonzola waves the Cress flag with what was irrelevant to Tom's stately rag. Tom has no time for shine, he grows his own salad. Gorgonzola is desperate to know who she is to embrace better development. If Gorgonzola could play darts she would be winning in the charts. Gorgonzola admires thunder, fault is the crack down. Gorgonzola listens to Irish music, she inherited Jason Donovan. Gorgonzola could have a less remarkable make over than Kylie, she'd just brush her hair. Gorgonzola opts for Shane McGowan, she's rougher than Terry Wogan where the young are. Shane McGowan gets drunk night after night like the smell of a skunk. Shane has a modern old man, twenty a few pints ago. The point of investigation suits Shane's song, he can. Modified secrets infect misunderstanding, that old man knows the truth. Old man has a friend called Jacob that sits in Esau's chair, he tells monologue to the place of air. Old man and Jacob run the board club, their advice is wanted. Shane is an Irish dissident that hallmarks Great Britain with folk bounce. Shane is very scruffy. The plight of Gorgonzola is most amusing with freedom fighting, amazed by accents. Gorgonzola socially flits. Wanted everywhere on the basis of Tom's career. Tom's wicked role on television plays itself out on Gorgonzola's pout. Gorgonzola has a prettier name but she is Nick to play pirates. Gorgonzola wonders around Camden when she is sixteen, relates bricks to the teenage point, place can go back. Gorgonzola didn't used to like Irish music that much until she realised about the ticket, could she get it. Distantly related to Shane, this means she's got an uncle in common. Gorgonzola is so related to success that she can only fail to fall in love. Gorgonzola thinks the chimney is her name, smell fire and money as they burn. Tom wants a role, what can this mean. Wish is useless to love and warn. Experience relevance, listen to Shane's song. Screaming scattered the cursed and fled. Pray to want more. Gorgonzola sings More! The old man dribbles for more, scribbles for more, diary lunch from nineteen forty four. Point about today is carriage for horse, have an ornament ahead of the car. Individuals no longer attain Whittington. Singular strife lasts as long as interview, who wants the stutter. Gorgonzola won't reside on any plank, she has her memory to chase. The old man belongs to the war's club, Gorgonzola is ten to one. Yahoo shout for fishermen, Gorgonzola thinks she's a marlin. Good slot for lead woman, she sings Doh Ray and despite all sex is then contained. Scumbag and maggot are toys for mythology. Belonging to third worlds. There are roles for Gorgonzola but she is a secretary to atomic filter. Gorgonzola loses her dreams in tuning up, she hears the widest sound crashing about and has to look up. Tom is in his cabin as a cabin boy. Cast a cabin boy. Punt. Tom is aware about bad language, he doesn't need words. When the television people tell their maximum the viewers can't expect tax return. Reality for earning living has staples and rulers and scissors. Dreaming is currently spinning, people should enjoy their time. Old man has more to get away from than Shane McGowan. Gorgonzola knows this. DJ is the applause store of constant celebration. This is the old man's ultimate goal. Favourites know how to. Old man has favourites in everyones, something that age takes to learn. Bias thwarts Gorgonzola with seeding futures she is tied with nearby shoe laces, doesn't think she's far away. Tom does have a name, not old man. Tom is jaunty from Gorgonzola's perspective, leather can spend in real terms. Let a circus what goes on in the old tavern, music runs till the end of the bar. Gorgonzola is the extent of American idiocy. Gorgonzola would laugh at a testicle. Trials of kids are scorned by Gorgonzola, she has lost her shadow. Sandwich applies that she is neither. Gorgonzola is most convinced by central navigation. Where's privacy from, the west end. Gorgonzola thinks she has the answer to treats, has musical talent. Most of the population are restricted to punk. Gorgonzola nods to all the traffic, doesn't know about swallowing garlic. How is the world brought up. eight o'clock breakfast over until lunch. Snacker bars and spit drops of paper espressos. Later ten o'clock when waters marginal break. Allowance for cyclists outdoors, tyre track surprise suit bottoms. Restless move from room to room, mark of glue and slouch. Hair from slack thinkers, prepare to slide. Gorgonzola looks into her chrome lamp, she has a modem that wouldn't comprehend. Old man surfs artillery and butterfly, gorgonzola has blink discloses thoughts to the floor. Old man practiced with his stick, Gorgonzola's children press arrow buttons. The old man left marks for the dog to chase, left places where leaves inter fact. Renovations reinforce Gorgonzola's playful choice, she imagines the DVD, they're showing a trampoline on two slabs of patio. Packet soup to everything enjoyment. Would like to drink milkshakes and chews too saucily into rosemary to be the guardian of tenderness. Old man doesn't swear like Gorgonzola, is better at composure. Gorgonzola looks to the day when she will enjoy a long run for the trio. Broadway, players have all had their day, but they're old men. Old man is older than seventy. How can old man and Gorgonzola meet in a story. Troops met with a beret. Gorgonzola met old man with immortality, she had hoped for money. Gorgonzola is irresponsible to thinks she is an old man. The End is Waltzing.

5
The Agreement

Action replenishes the level, symbiosis to disability. Absorbed claim to disinherit the tired fiasco. Double limit to salvage the wound. Perplexity absteins from worth, setting the ride to need. Mettle fill a luxurious compromise, button sour address to attend suction. Finish rate of circumspect account, endure respite. Loan for temperament form, fixative argument. Despite loss, instant course raise let. Sheltered burn besides, the impetus to segregate. Younger things resolve ways for high protection. Sadness enjoys muddle to preach astride brand, parent nurture exact carts. File paper in wallet, prevail draw. A giving mind perceives to lose resilience. Tough pleasure fix hearsay. Selfish pipes of sending signals, extrapolating fight as a form of logic. At arms length masses pile, velvet forms of translation. Good port so to speak, parts well. Term those times to overlap. Refresh good spare word, secret thing to guard. Thus fortress among gong, historic component sit and learn. Thatch from what was done, billions entertain line. Present day a man at hand, luggage reserve pairs. Other way three o'clock, metaphor to tack down. Prism assess surface noise share. Proportions range to contemplate, resemblance with conclusion. Matter to purge, lest appearance know. Persons frightful reward. Spoons crook a glance, becoming strangers of their leisures. Forced to be appraised for vacuums. Fancy a thing to be plain. Loved and infected for clothes. Surround sense repair distance. Run ways to keep clear. Exception in realm to talk of. Blithe exchange in petty rate. Discussed stalling vagabond for pilgrimage. Let sleep endure sufferance, instinct prey upon leverage, progress dismayed to slump in choice. True gain a martyred form to pause cares for shillings. Less size for animals, cuddles and abattoirs. In patience months put. Further apprehension soothe. Schooling appoint horse to bend. Swear carriages to guide course. Blame correct hand bag, strapped in tales by design. Become of a furlong to win. Court from a beastly resource. One day wake wood entree, whittle flutes. Storyless breathe on the lifeless. Complaint exact term of worry, headache include position. Disclosure rework events, no record wears despondence. Portion of health a proven tune. Intellect bejewel weary hen with scrambled eggs. Verse a champion for deaf ears. Apparent success of blind tolerance, overseer to all spectacle. Revulsion warp elation. Custom hops pros and cons. Mediating the pane that satisfies. Cauldrons name this Inverness with two friendly ladies to interpret. Lather winter pass as summer, benefit doubt for milling chips. Restrain the answer to gander yonder, constrain 'the'. Erase take form. Write to leave the snare. Mentioned thus a matter worse to price force. Vow that fades, often was with correlation. Wrong man name right sign. Listener challenge tune to overpaid. Irony is clumped on top, schooling banter claim the hob. Joke in red shoes, appoint distraction. Concentrate falser pitch. Read measures bounty on physique. generous twitter muted with something wrong to excel from. Muse abandoned song for scolding. Vulcher in a clever chair, copying from care that idolises.

6
Nottingham

1 packet of felt pens
1 mug of hot chocolate
1 alarm clock
1 pair of sunglasses
1 bottle of water with bacon roll meal from Burger King
1 shadow 1 bus
1 meal on Friday night
1 conversation about labour
1 man with psychopathic tendencies
1 bench with tables and spilt Coca-Cola
1 party after another
1 group of smiling people
1 idea that outdoors is better
That car is marvelous. It looks colourful
1 man that looks similar

1 lady laughing
1 sausage with a sesame bun only ketchup not chili
1 fair with trampolines
1 church in Nottingham Four bottles of London pride
1 view of rooftops, and the city
1 chestnut tree with conkers
1 National Express
1 box of orange Ribena
1 packet of Walkers crisps
1 DAB digital radio
1 Pitcher and Piano
1 cup of cafe latte 1 Mozart's Requiem
1 tickle on the nose
2 men touch their noses
2 black men
1 man lost on the tube Going to Whitechapel
1 man says take the lift
1 girl doesn't pass on stairs
1 comedy evening
1 Rastafarian with a friend
1 CD 1 program of News Night
1 packet of salt n vinegar
1 bar that serves Mad Dog Half a pint of Guinness instead Jesse
Jackson on News Night
1 man offers a seat on the bus Quiet and usually guilty
A mumbled thank you
1 mobile phone dropped On the floor of Bread and Roses
1 set of rundown batteries
1 loop without open tobacco
1 man that says 'District' Can be found that way.
1 Swiss army knife.
1 tickly nipple.
1 person that comes from Yorkshire.
People that aren't failed. Wrong thoughts going to
Nottingham. Coming back again. Looking trigger through.

Short ones like dark faces presume. Phoenix nights are universities. Dipping elbows in beer. Laughing hard keep in touch. Check in the afternoon. Check out at a minute to eleven. Cafe for smoking. Camp shop a tent. Kendal mint cake. Handkerchief not choosing. Repeating to remember closing paths. Scurrying to sit down and look away. Impertinently agreeing to be wrong. Marveling at danger. Seeking repeating it. Electing self to bear. Mantle Queen's wand. Orient title dinners with re-runs of light comment. Very subtle you knows. Tiny hints, even spots. Computer system cracks on virus crashers, Security hacking. Choosing a loo in a dungeon. Flushing to leave a bit. Heavy shopping. Vegas second chance. Black square of paper. Busy city bustle. Deserted street looking up blonds. Worrying darkness. Obliging sympathy. Seeing scratchy noses As signs of racism. desirable agent A baseball cap. Loops and Barren escalators. Air conditioning strips. Long vision across a room. Black felt tips. Chocolate in Star Bucks. Not enough change. The Perth Ball. Not inviting Sweating and hotness. Taking the lift. Watching lift doors. Broken train, information Thinking. Mad Dog Czech relations in castles. Europeans hanging statesmen. Grey currents of river tide. Eleven fifteen seeing the hairdresser. Because of Yorkshire reading The Sun. Shrinking from the bar Shrinking near the end. Resorting to the loo. Keeping to self obstinacy telephoning stars. Turning cards waiting for shots. Placement resignation dumb soliloquy. Gathering for drinks Associates in. Face references. Similarity within chins. Setting alone defiant searches. Beckoning recognition. Sad because it matches. Another clash trauma. Convict escape to fields with mooing cows. Shun the smile to prove what. Only one funny understanding. Fat man with sexy eyes and tribe that eat special ice-creams. Don't miss off-beat or shirk or hide the finding. Explosive faces humiliate Outraged. Wiser to marshall sordid girl for a full belly Popping ear plugs. Trancing gadgets notice birds catching tunes like worms, bugs, beetles.

Shop thresholds for Blondie. Queen and Simon Le Bon Circuit Buying pause. Porter shortage While Melinda sports a head of straw. Bequeathed brain. Synchronised crossing roads. Answering junctions. Staving faulty To melody and Harmony. Ascribing luggage for accurate depositions. Always surmounting gala to simple action. It doesn't hurt to think without begging. Smart insult funny smack. No CD for a round. Slip off track most slippery, juice and potato types of success through windows. Congested traffic steering wrongly. Laughing too soon when drowning. Phew arrogance. Aligned to misadventure. Permanent casting on train of enquiry. Boxed to present. Prize of discovery. Cancerous blots dot the mind. Carpet hope encounter cleaners. Low beings blowing cover appearing. Turning up at exit nine all over again. Orange bag day of sequence. Prophet's dial buy pair of white sox. Blunder spells vaguely entertaining. Second time round goat. Own adventure pleasing definite. Hair like rosemary. Religions of population. Well direction steeply calm. Repose rehearsing dreams. Approach demi gods turning ankles. Foggy overheads Overwhelming reads. Packets accepting blag notices. Sticking teachings of surroundings. Speaking international to chat shows. Trait taboo in souvenirs. Edge base pantomime. Expenses in perpetration Fetching lessons. Commentary on both sides. Questioning answers back and forth districts. Hammersmith, Barons Court, Hammerbaron Acronyms, hooking fish With bait, not catering. Leaving flu behind with vitamin duffel coat. Donkey monitor credit in clean person. Dirty habit bogus. Travel habituating cleanliness. Soapy lilac, fruity fresh baby. Peering eyes on pure and just anger. Simple beautiful faith. Deserving walks rounded. Pen drop flag company. Beaten retreats Without urgency. Plain order in human mistakes. Thirst meeting time thankfully. Reassurance sticking prejudice. Ironic that so and so is a politician. Spooky probably catch a parade. Vilified guess serenely. Depreciation cover outright tool. Noble fascism modest performance. Quilt as if the effort. Access dead line chord. Powerful blood mimic saving purchase. Mother step in puddles. Plod in attack ripple cheating sky. Clear views from stagnant glass. Clan dune without lizards. Marsh grass hosting evolution in practical jokes. Specs and surname witness brother affection. Inscribed with possible to love tennis and croquet. Thinking that Jack can play in a garden at school. Ambition to meet Jerry Springer Widen protocol. Glean global entourage. Big mystery stage futures With hot press. Peculiar foreign policy with intimate address. Chop a willy like a ham bun. Cookie exchanged for twenty pences. Fork for a spoon. Rounded scotch egg. Overhead copper spot beam under cover. Night surveillance swivel commentary. Benjamin Bitten write a hand brake turn. Divert and covet cigarette. Break in packs of ten. Swoon scrambled egg inside a fortress. Castellate in drags for plumes of smoke. Butts collecting conjugation. Mass filtration. Pringle jumper pop a crisp. Brims o'er culminate whims. Asbestos and margarine, Petty France loops in franchise. Horse guards and parades for Betty at home. Hot bath prices per head. Group spilling foils. Silver cloud the aluminum. Cranes of axle nodding donkeys. Bent elbows climbing stairs. Watch from the tower close the bridge. Echo birds draw burrowing. Borrow the float down a river on a log. Pointing tribes. Either side regatta at Gryffindor. Wand hand. Left click mouse parcel. Conglomerate Stick mention Lego brick to Ego dick. Explain give up down town. Curio pause. Bye bye limousine. Eat pork chemically. Guess yesterday. No one words enough script Intelligence. Superstition feel hot beaches with lotion. Kiss an old maid. Poem enterprise MOD. fugue after two beers. Serum prides evening lie. Which way coast south. Aye That way! Manners of span. Shivers appointing rain. Magnificence of sea at wide ports. Large boats and congress. Points at fault. Half a sister half. Council for the blind. Gaze on same rose. Rivals weaving constant bones. Scores of how parents slap. Squabble the job bare. Onion burn guard instrument. Over used mash potato. Gum bashing milk slopping. Try some cream. Thoroughly unpleasant to a cold extent. Nurture of idealism for children. Importuned with hypothetical envy by long separations. Thirteen margins of glitterati. Holidays for eldest privilege. Familiar network against failure. Obsolete jungles of television. Coarse dances of shy ways. Wish treachery on Miss Endeavor. Affairs and house parties left out. Wrong foot amuse misbehaved. Sincerity hold compromise. Fact promise pastry. Marshaled with indifference. Half town deciders. Litigation wire opinion. Learn consequence from bastions. Resembler of good life. Quit knowledge half percentage. Individuality grow loneliness. Section mighty tool. Bar tend migrating pool. Cope with love invitations. TV dinner. Come as you are. Better without a shag. Overhear stare at communist days are over. Patronage to cheery groups. Accusing fun of having them. Inquisition Scottish people. Prouder than a sore debate. Led curfew to a border. Queen queer sanctuary. Chances like saying No, hate Carmen. Being able to find the right flip flops. Visiting Pasadena's in east London. Driving there to eat melon. Piece With blue. Chain of building plans for match funding. Convenient not hindsight. Missing a lift with transport. Pedophile waiting next term. Offering lives to small children. Tall Magic in duress. Careless grinding. Could be disgusting places. Pink pants and green dresses going large with warren. Real on demand. Cornered every room. Nonchalance coy part. This is house of God. Weapons have no place. Servant of written down. Replay no ransom paid. Take holiday Tickled cheek. mother intervene to insult her child. Mild protection to like the lad. Slow chap. Chubby in the arms. Traveling horse Pass confession. Mask jibe or Green chronicles. Late night telly glowing orbs. Rope men at tree sides. Misty end in proffered pen. Seems okay. Quick read passing next line. Character trend less hip than shooting. Garland trinket at Trelawny Wells. Keep fully charged with concern. Cohesion string of albums. Gizzard Men in white robes. Float raft swim ashore by plunging. Glug and gloop swallow whole fish. Dissenting thirsts to a tiled floor. Woodland dwarf laze Sunday afternoon. Sequins of armor throw away clothes. Take this and return! Shut brothers under skin. Terrible peas in the freezer Like Gary Glitter. Seventies retro feather. Fighter ships picking nostrils. Far enough wrong for Elton John. Fight or die where to stand. Gold a blazing furnace. Keep a walking Western front. Chesapeake Hawk in sky. Memphis Saves the west end snow storm in a dome. Found the sort of power. Furnish aim tackle for solid trust. Bench plain manner stick faults. Streamline shunty pole. Prism encounters before hand outs. Change job in variety. Method double sided. Good in a chair. Not worst best. Tart and pastry Bit. Trigger tease paint tapes and grappling. Swap orangutan from what was said. Excellent fruit flies and rare morning. Noon going up as flying prey. Good view skyline someone else. Write and have it read. Thought of stolen shared at the same time. Shake budgerigar by the hand. Perching number tens. Lending scores next ounce. Analysis Cribbing cheer ups. Cast wake that's all. A long brilliant night. Jeopardy enrich with practice. Getting civil rewards in company. Spoon and fork get home from thunder. Stay dry miss the rain. Watch it pelt reach home. Open match wash up wet. Marigold stay dry but start again. Rain after storm not tropical. Just wet Washing spins over. Buckets and flashes. Boring rumbles rolling crashes. Pitter patter isn't watch. Have to be there. Experience telling reference. Effect sharing would be. Story page of print reporting. Accuracy stalled.

7

Long John Silver

John stares with silvery ways. Pacing the stage in vibrant dress. Clasping swords and jumping on his bendy knees. Long John holds hands with cutsey. Drinks bottoms up savvy benign. Tortured with best, he wears a tight shirt in burnt skin. Dyed hair and worry completely capital of going. Watches jerking round sixties pedestrian crossings. Assignations with cream. Thoughts of Polly. Nasal blind observances following gongs. Polly shares advert hymns belted from lowly caves. Silver John fishes in the dark Black quays. Film romp for measured men like silver John. Bead sweat according age. Goodness oppression guards have upset Polly. When beasts know shame. Silver John might know. Questions in Polly's mind. Bobbing along to silver John Eaves in walls. Scratchy ears of hunger and slaughter. Leaden men tears shopping for bargains. Mistaken breeze wafting hair poles. Little flutters. Ripple flag on pirate ship. Crisp bracket with treasures on cross bone palms. Liquored spoon the rasp. Tongue lolling for proms. Cussing land about coconuts. Brie in giant melons and peach. Silver John is Currency of bad wind for a quiet bay. Shovel tarnish cross wet hands in bag slings. World back risk excitement on virgin plan development. Ruminate on Long John's boat. Steers in solutions of lovely things on cruel women. Middle age men of mystery. Plant on younger solace. Beet root in a sanded pit. Spilling soup on naked arms. Apple pie instead. Some is waste alternate. Spoof the accident casting away. Haste of port from Cardinal Hume. Under arm Head lodged On a brick stern. Silver John puzzles.

Cleaving midgets. Outback wing marveling vein experiment. Decide to test Long John and Silver John. John Silver and silver. John Silver long with Silver John. John long with Silver John. Long silver with Silver John. John John with silver John. Long with silver John.

Silver John bleaches his hair. Seems unfair in numbers or experiment. Occurring accident hardly precedent. Cigarette butts pile into. Smoke to silver John Long reminisces Fireside. Song Silver John Comes walking by From his chopper full of virgins. Papyrus handsome. Cuticles nipped and arms brazen. Dashboards of Sonnet screens. Formula brides for earthen worms. Goose pimples to cheeky smiles. Carnivals of stoke turns. Big fetch of gaiety. Quality stares of jeopardy lying in balms. Silver John is terribly at home in the world disco. Nasturtium coife for tune moods. Marsupials and bat men convalescing. Care homes salutation armaments. Bid no buts. John Against smoking Says. Silver John Outnumbered by Bad habits. John silver packet of silver to silver John. Harmless Distribution. Nickel paper engine dime. Silver John reads palms. Everyone knows gypsy. Hiding turn From news. Cinema goer business pains. Charm Crash about wet slug shell. Smoke a bad idea. John of a silver bush. Cormorant canopies of warming feeling. Comfort yellowing bowls of Anthisan and Dextrose. Boost flag at nineteen holes. Dark ages can Decorate trees At Christmas. With hair and baubles Silver John strands tied pieces. Found confession right about what Pope says. Women men fighting. Silver John buffs up well behind ears of knighting caption articles. Without hyperactivity. Obvious not busy. Get on the bus at just invisible. Leave home bridle youth with suffering. Imaginary pass on learning. Strike match forget. Said is for passengers. Pitch comes home from branding. Tossing hay may be old fashioned. Extremely charming in picture. Left handed to right Chameleon with shaking different times ways. Horses drinking coke pools. Ideas barrels of tears. Sherry caskets street muskets. Shopping the floor. Uncollected wards. Decide not detest. Silver John's virgin Intent. Experiment decide then marriage. Celebrate mobile phones. Lose concord planes floating balloons. Clown getups ramming sheep. Dipping ticks. Sweet corn mashed potato. Fluffy in ways. Extra terrestrial witty cues. Red dwarf canaries. Pylon Pilate very religious. Hill sound Gold spot. Blue Spot dog. Quick silver evermore silver. John Makes pastry. Only rain glistens on silver John's hair. Fronds of bracken steal pylons. Fort Savlon grid. Boat under bride. Tides recede.

Think he was the piano player of choice. Really eat the smarties. Middle of the road. Marjoram flea spaghetti junctions. Pompeii Jackson hole on holiday. Osbourne's on TV. Jewish wedding. Superkalafragragilisticexpialadotious. Smarties answers. Stag comes out the bracken with moss all over his horns. Sees a few people like me and then carries on eating. Fur come off his antlers from scratching bark and he looks like a warrior with bits dangling off. Fur like skin that sways off his antlers. Sees a fawn and drinks from the trench of water. Happy gets in to cool off. Stands for a while and then drinks, scratches his back. A while later he crosses to the other bank and heads for thistles. Man with two carrier bags and probably his wife walk past. Borders bookshop Waitrose. She has a fishing bag. Word 'academic' heard in passing. There was a lovely blue dragon fly before they came along. Someone on his own. Boy in bright orange has a shoulder height stick. Footsteps together hold hands. Keys in the pocket. Curly haired girl with a water bottle that needs filling up. Tree, three fairies, their dad, a spaniel, parents hand in boy and girl, wheat germ. Bob Harris cement, half a beer. Cracking sixty years on educated choice. Green felt pen. Fitting to engine squeaks. Flag wave the fiddle bombs. Ptolemy And Mary Anne driving home to red light runs. Summer cancer war. Inscrutable belching scrums. Handy note in restorations. Old men strategies are not implemented. Good. Bawdy louts with nipples hanging out. Patriotic at desk tasks. Radio always learning. Turf foundation homeward bound. Two racing Putney bridge on Sunday. Drink of water at The Mitre. Pointless escapade for men in red suits. Chelsea wink at a medal. Grand sustenance handful from Millions. Fallen always close shaven. Tiny action kicking handbags. Bumper parking outside the hairdresser. Channeling in for better reception. Media clues in views. Other people's decision in a baseball cap. Thinking does The Queen sit down. Not crying for Slipping back. Hot feeling denim. Grubby toes on green bed expenditures. Pacify star burst that did it in strawberry. Cope on circle black with lightning. Coincidence Fine the peer group mould. blood a dime Of pound and spend. Mirrors unfolding For people to die. Felt pens running out. Monophycytism blinis with Vache Qui Rita Taramasalata . Pesto goat in tortellini. Duke red face. Skin burnt flank of snatching horn. Lowering white behind the door. Bunker epigram. String who shot the story. Pitch curmudgeon squelching wrathful corns. Quango morta. Barney hip the repair. Intimate Castaway disabled creed. Convolute ordinary things. Respect is full of gratitude. Shackle Deciphering sentries. Impede X burning eager with desire. Dinner after scrabble. Husband own dorm. Captain bandage underfoot. Food raid Neat bedspread. Partnership canopy. Jailer sharing rods of hospitality. Sickened green mountain. Fables crowded rocks. Can't help stick tightly. Severely unique. Reverse Beckon a dance. Once a year counts. Parade in jackets and flags. Tribute sport home. Speed in motion going to fridge. Bounce taking weekdays. Wine on Fridays with TV Ear. I love you friends eating decorums. Together fables. What's on off the difference. Gold and silver spitting hose. Not turn round. Sofa primary pastel. National tragedy in strike. Match over shoulder. Walk on the wild Liberia. Struggle keep up. Republic address subtitles. Plague taught uncertainty skins. wave arm Kevins from Disney teams. Four and two Mauritius on tarmac.

Britain is the Motown founder of Athens's Galaxy. Chocolate Lincoln's Inn meet sailor. Dignitary suit size sixteen. Come to terms with grown. Flow feature crowning flux. Plays in politic adult. Subject few geometry. Pythagorus discard. Youth move spreadsheet. Correspondence minor skip. Patch downing company. Torch bon soire en chansan drug. Nosey lose precedent. Must love first says counter on table. Leg prefer tripod, plan four. Cereal foil silver spoon. Dipping little bowls and large glands With flakey corns. Currently in possession Of Baron Stump John. Chop with a hand held propellor fan. on a string Choobacca shell. Hand bag the car door. Get out one way. Cotton wool not allowed. St. Paul break bond of organ concert. leaving early passing front. Noisy blunder jilt a twinge .steal against exodus. Religion choosing strolled embankment. India then Israel Lollipop Union Jack. Tourist direction away. sin deliver The Lord. Barrier against walking out. Exercise encounter man. Salute glass summary. Afternoon in Holiday Inn. Ex patriot guide a station. Bangladesh diplomacy Champions. build a man like granny. Adieu America cross plus. Romeo Juliet Rome and Greater Missenden. Bit bobs. Not looking stupid By a statue. Train left along sidewalks where none stand. But cyclists small girl in hair band. Fidget mop cotton to face. Interpret rude behaviour. Blond hair childlike. Sincerity taking leave. Crypt the dome daylight. Stained glass grandeur. Envy entrapment difficult enough float the course. Jerking rebellion Small indignation. Everywhere tested armored Disinheritance. choosing defeat All martyred Backward. Youth overgrown. Butterfly tattoo a piggy back ride. Mind that child whip cream van. Eros gaze. Phlegm omelette. Sticky pudding paper strewn. Tabernacle knock castle gate. Flinch light slam sun stream. Gaunt letter is done with accusation. Inconclusive measure matador wandering. Judge uncreased face. Fertility's tide. segment of lime chime Broadway. Slum advertising move the clothes. Double decker busy magic. Read souls buy circuit messages. Grout failure with sublimity. Aggressive detention mildly formed. Must love a loathed enemy says Juliet. Parent with quarrel companion. Pure silver Candles. Penny pewter ring. Name of part belonging man. Name of sword clash resonance. Defense guilt In silent thought. drags of smoke. Fiery plane Fan Car exhaust. Pollution unwashed beast. Dust prone season moving pasture. Love from love school. Tarot engross conversation. Twiddling thumbs pedestrians. Re-trod streets. Walkabout conviction Without destination. Chance entertaining scraps. Sharp solution ugly man. Shiplake Mortlake. Both lakes. Point on great gramophone. Music bash vandalise. Mercutio dead for supper. Water box of cherry. handgun drop pellet with man rain. Wail enforce law. Faith in love. Insatiable where passion cuts. Action past wandering flip flops. Inaccurate daily task. Explain fault with clumsy un plaiting. Ravel half thrown yo-yo. Wind up clutch day. sequence left turn. Aggravate slope. Escalate grave wrongly punctuated. Close home child. Unstop touch, motioned beside the Japanese. Comparable pig went oink. Profile caught proudly. Quick negotiate blame. Notice inch. Match Circe's impression. Enemy team identity fix. Promise salutation. Introduce house in well kept history. Debate keeping seen. Robson Jerome professional Christian. Towards end conclusion. Every moment bind spiral. Blood drawn affection birth. Spilt for small grazes. Knocks bruising check dimension. Obstacle with pain ties. Feature leaving annual spate. Unbuttoning autumn's cool nudity. Chestnuts like other english plants. Don't defeat the under sitters with more than broken skin. Dinners in hard wood. Small flat soft mansion of love. Television fade soft book of pulp. Page flicker. Embolden words of Technicolour. Fare of brevity. Applause haul brick wall. Concert of The Channel. midday Without grip attentions. tedium long way round. Ring mop bottom glasses. Leave marks for skidding hoops. Panty line rape alarms. Fall axis box ironing board. Skirt past twelve forty. Self confessional actions that string hoards. doubt Doubled over, feast pork and mean lies. Jolly string sausages. Knotted tie a milky bar. Gymnast fling a symmetry. Egging grip the disappointment. Reward horizon stable. Broad coloured for dull sky censure. Recharge moan. Beano sniff old game. Rule of picket fence. Failure greet red nose. Seeping gently from brown to red. Move unsubscribed. Placement skittish platter. To be weighted, scaled judge curtailed. Spelt out by jack knaves. Periwinkles or enslaved. Today is an old argument stung with learning. Instance yarn absolving. Dismiss 'perhaps' as a science. Later mistake posting. Route squares among shares. Short perfection with yearly spreads. Identikit earl seized by one hundred dons. Tweezer commentary as fashion promises to be interesting. Thatcher Travel card lop zones. Roof pouched in a steward's tabard. Rose in a plastic cup. Could have been a glass vase. Drinking ear wax and small flies from a bin. Empty the name drops. Jest after cold shower. Ring time warp in discussion. Plastered is cleaner. Form dressed by two pm. One thirty emperor, redwing coach. Strathmore BLT. No recorded tour guide. Circuit a palace room. Hanoverian Butterflies over tennis. Cabbage patchers handling doors as benches. Cigarette Mown grass. Lazy foot print run down a battery. Blooming photo guide a hand. Obsolete enclosure fair. Fountain outdoors. Tug of gilded iron. Apron in string, knock a disaster. Overcast light with lesbian kiss. Mothers on despair. chided from pointing. Elder spirals down. Issuing tickets. Reimburse carriage cantankerous. Obstinate clog swerve mercury. Silver epicentered to swivel eyes. Expedition Olympic dot. Hopkins benching. Wednesday's Monday to Friday. Lone mile from Los Angeles. Belvoirbrook dress multiplex. Jupiter Recycling plastic arrows to paths. Jane with Horrocks Microphones. First class travel clean design. Decisive action. Vestibule permission for men in cabinets. Postcards choosing higher wages. Over hedge brim over treads. Spindle of yew charting blind. Forge me knot wilderness tapestry. Threads defer ignorance. Enclosure to syllabus. Curriculum off amazement. Maze another episode Of Michael Portillo investigating. Policy rights of research. Chip last conclusion to magic the program. Counterfeit a favourite song. Protect insult from showing off Contender of brave countenance Innovate like to repeat. New custom in the maze Cell wall from birth to death Cell print footsteps Garden thicket fetch screen shade From Madderty To Dundee Defend something that had. Slip under in gravity Road and seated tarmac Covering ground in the same present sun Omni will not face again. Stubborn profile set the August bank holiday. Hot coal bleed with a leech. Scouring upbeat about skin conditions DT 4015 Digital camera competition. PO Box 2029 B299 7XU. Human cabinet younger than brand. Older than emulate Shrug off backwards. Leaning performance husk strawberries. Acidic joints from Coca-Cola. Blurb on delivery. Long toenail. Sticky surface building dust. Relief settle week stiles. Solitaire pegging frailty bribes. Masturbation theme tunes of missed chance. Training behind them X certificates Passing incy wincies. All the best rules near trap doors Whoops a daisy Flutes on geriatric news. Non salivation click back the car seat. Not dropping copper pennies for silver. Sandwich hint against the clock. Carrot of hatching chicks. Gobbling worms for bread crumb poisons. Champions to fledgling treats. Boxed parentage high on a wall. Golf ball swung suspenses. Make forces or tenderness. Care for budgerigars with millet. Picture of a nun without a bridge. Tall stack a doormat. Encryption the sole. Boot threading home and away. You can be that plan. Casts of bus drivers. Omen lingering doubt. Conclude cycles with no break. False chip negotiating drunken streams. Sobriety Where knobs cook. Feasible paths of snatch. Perverting umbrage sophistication. Self paralysis enamoured. Consider keep low level. Underground enemy bound up. Trojan kicking dust with red laces. Unobserved wombles with loud music at desk jobs. Idols of brooding single dinners. Self promotion harmony at Saturday's rock. Vote for

style's request. Savage in spot lit Bunty. Animate across the hill.
Pitch for grass. Blade chew cud at human faculty. Galas of wit
for marshalling sprains. Caress flair. Burgeon debt in grace.
Confound wayward sleuth. Spirited with every lie. Breaks in
mental give way. Spot decipher crossword. Without help is
miraculous. Copy cat Incidents that creep into toast. Cereal
affect jam on sale because trench coats glue the air with fixing
story. Sorrow vacuously explained. Wiser glimpse crave fat.
Kind man authentic processor. Guardian of precious juggle.
Frond colour the shard. Kevin Costner Fridays. Portrayal never
meant frozen. But the nymphs played And wrestled.
playground balls For crystals. Scrape factors of advancement.
Peer lash hero to sleigh. Clamp doric columns with mantles.
It's where you're seated. Budge up old dame. Stage wonder
with miserable loans. Debt like chum yearns. Plonkers I have
missed. Eloise in corner of highest pavilion. Butterflies
digitally attracted. Lift a sorry child. If herpes leans. Flavour on
morose Phlegm. Cowed misinterpreted. Betty nude steps in.
Time to roll. Tip timber Shaven to carpentry. Old crow's beak.
Ears roses. Toes noses. Thorn prick thorn near ear. Very
strong in prevention. Imbue trap with autumn leaves. Drop a
penny catch a taxi. Curb a gutter in guessing. Quite the wash.
Scourge of friends at stolen dreams. Together camp in
warehouses. Same of the toothbrush. Used not the same.
Drops of spilling Leaves. I grew in saturated copper sulphate.
Back and get the crystal. Know an errand for sharing. Head for
disembodied. Fervour where to hide.

8

Wanted to meet Ralph Fiennes so. Followed Freud's play Down clackety clack. At the end was a Blind man who led by Penny Farthing. Dusk market in sadness tatters. Place lost in scum mistakenly. Honest with blight because it shut down. Absolutely years ago. Blind man behalf.

Troll stick navigate share. Among but sprites live. Sliver chance of scolding. Normal doubt intrigue. Expire like yoghurt mould. Hoick spoon off. Relish spare relish. Mold mould Before. Lichen stone. Pliability bun. Consider kilns at high degrees. Discovery But, with but for breakfast. Food transform hypocrisy. Giles for goats that milk. Cheese is for bacteria. Sort it out then. Learning pickets me from thee. Bouncing laps with drumstick Bones. Bloods of sisterhood. Approve a society gaited for lobby. Rail approach eight too early. Clink Hampton Court. Sausage race maze. No-one but 'today' to visit the maze. Overcast fauna. Miss the other years. Carve a fortress. Apparently visit apparently. Thirty pick the lids of smarties. Look for the dog called Fergus. Call everything Fergus. Eat a hot dog for the hell of it. Try out sugared mustard. Tackle haze in debonair. Still need a DJ. Clouds for a break of sun because it shines. Florida as a genuine option for a Kingston garden. Tackily dethroned by privet allowance. Speciality alliance condition. Yes press back to front. Label inset with the rustic table. Hang a man in beams. Princess cup and sword sir. Condition of sincerity watches the court of history. Yesterday inconvenience. Load and vice arrived. Handling overtly. Bad pack dry not wasting. Persisting growth in crucifying. Exact words that should be a blessing, no goldfish. Mirrors at fairs. In and Out changing dues. Arabian nights on the power of happiness. Jonathan moon a cinema tree.

Spoon a tooth. Highers belong to themselves. Self possession for wonders. Disowned mistakes on hearts. Apple cores from pithy natures. Contrive spell on course. Earning learning blood and oxygen. Words heated or schooled. Strings unbowed and sounding bored. sultan with Geronimo. Shield from brilliance and failure. For what for. To go by in conversation. Fighting as bears on weaponry. Sordid wit not right. Admonished thinking is hard. Better standard Of health and well being. Surpass to fit. Equation for porn. Dim sloth wiring. As if it were my junction. Barbecue arranged but sausages burned. Wisdoms overturned. Cups handling perfumes. Breather stale in periphery. Glum for the blush Overriding Concealment. Blurred shades of slim line. Faction. What should I worry about. Aston Villa's David O'Leary's equality. Stepping aside big boys for small boys. Feeling abide. big as boys girl. Membership club Mosquito. Swat recycling beautiful bush. Signal rite of summer for summer people. Can't keep count of temperate. Scorches. Mildew and greenfly. Blossom band for gardener. Sulker brood again. Green shield stamp. Husk with twixt nail. Read at birth. Reader by the reader. Publish pasture futures like a Spaniard. How it can rectify. Procession Leicester. Square cartons neon heights. Topiary flutes ear shots. Stall street three chirps. Triangle slotted shapes. Restrain them bulging. Steeples piled on hopeful troops. Bits and pieces candied reward. New dress through cameo. Deference without a bow. Plaid requisitions. Waltz over a canyon. Fish swim wear. Penguin dive twenty thousand LPs. Sequence chartered with clementine. Thugs brighten internationally. Unit rooms village squares. Castanets round fires and sleeping geraniums. Conquistadors on south seas. Discounted in shorter breaks. Pepperoni selling vegetarians as drum sticks. Oasis drink a camel. Flakes. Smokey plumes in Brighton. Mistaken bad for manners. Lady shoelace catching a hazel nut. Insurrection not peaches and cream. Photo of cream. Wheelchair in roulette. Catches of a falling nut. Molar chew brittle taste.

Never say thank you. To you. Not Ten years ago. Never
Allowed myself Forgiveness. Would not have known the
words for blame. Shuttle judgment aggrieve to settle. Both
hopes churn under one that did again. to tee the flotsam.
Plank Low pressure. Brannigan pastry in Schweppes bitter.
Judge forgiveness to understand. You may be God But so is
everyone else. You may be tied by a strand of hair. Clipped back
from Boots. Next shampoo in scratch. Ointments As modern
remedies go. Shelf lives mending round ones. Dog on a lead
left on a slab. Watch knees bend up High Streets. Powerful
universally. Pray for themselves on your behalf. Feature meet
past. Spear mystery fight the soldier. Yoke of breakfast egg.
Good for adventure post this way. Shock badger, side with set.
Amount left to the finger. Rolling paths of grain. Giant spine
from hand to arm. Plain chair in forgery. Help liturgy crack
symphony. Actual path virtual phrase. Blue Peter ZADiOC.
Dead people are coming back to important times. Elvis cleaves
the perennially drunk. Nostalgia with measure. Not brained
Equally. Decade of mass anecdote. Adjective license. Conclude
rite. Sister drop bounty. Cheeseburger chomp hungry. Absent
minded snacking. Glamorously Bejeweled. Flip flop wrap
a skirt. Artificial shopping ten pm's way home. Hot little
slice. Greaseproof wrap. Embezzle for bold things. Chance of
bung. Store young men in caps from China. Mop in strident
day. People filing. Pass on fruit and vegetables. Dribble
muncher. Holiday brunch dot globally. Giant 'M's of yellow
Marry. Pret a Manger prawn and lettuce. Fresh ingredient
silver law. Good practice working. Itch and Tingle greed not
price. Early departures scooting off grinding paste. Swallow
vice in fizzy straws. Knobbledy with carrot juice. Fanta next
improvement. Words for onion rings. Partials of caramel
black. Vice president consider attraction. Election soar eagles
on the Spey. Cranny gilded chook. Bald un feathered pants.
Gawp binoculars collecting eggs. Feast their eyes. Danny The
Champion of the World. Crack tiny sticks under trainers.

Truffle skim stones with nanny pledging ripples. Mirage in compliment. Bicker longevity. Angelic foster strains of lyrical tongues. Cue advance homily. Know a beef sand witch. Dainty in fragile bitch. Feet drag up rags. Smoke spires blow weather vane. House one sky. Chimney pot vertical pip. Spoke mast rooves. Bottled bunion domes. French widow French window. Turret Gargoyle humming perfumes. Smokey bakery toiletries. Pigeon mess on warm slate. Bitch twist bunch of stems. Chewed lie mend fracture. Gaping hole fantasy. Window and shaft. Not a builder but a jostler of men. Align prune to stone a gateway. Sheared waist in hard caps. Chisel and tong minding shelter for better that bitch would like To be. Obvious church in crystal esplanade. Pave Jonathan Cainer. Starry host templing bodies. Before and after cremation in sycamore leaves. Crumble rumble bright day. Unbred to parentage of flower. Daisy ton in meadow. Style to children's hair. Bitch past seeing. Rhododendron and wild blossom. Coursing trample country streets. Litter lawn protect institution. Good gospel pounds. Plenty fish on office walls. Netting profits of Mademoiselle B. Correction stave wholesome enterprise. Life's industry of wit. Switch engagement parcel discharged. Love unleash from puritan shelter. Gothic sepulcher. Green house of tomato. Packet soup pillar. Bank lobby a hallway. Monkey sachet. Incense with safety. God bless you mobility. Dance a flute. Jolly bonk wooden floor. Step squeak in gate. Hinge a plaintive turnover. Fashion accessorise torpid. Milk over laconic. Tragedy spake from a green eye. Den Monday choose Wednesday. Week per head. Party in lost dance. Scratch string a future in bed. Karma sutra. Stub toe for tapping cash. Debenham's garb one Saturday on. Saturday lamb in a Greek restaurant. Plate next door. Balloon debate no argument . Just cash I do. Distribution agendas, purchase orders, telephone messages. Contract of friendship hardship. Negotiate same diary. Dinner at one in plausible fare. Minestrone housing office. Place is mine. Street left turn. Jackie waits with patience.

Blobby wears a hiding. Signal round class chance. Gloomy woomy latex paint. Golden Smile crisps. Casual mortgage state. Yeah corner nice date. Pretty address a chimney. Personality flaming temps. Agency fee chopping wood. Tie knot Monopoly mind. Map staff soot. Thick above hearth. Old bliss fit shoe. Pick like planet Ron. Said you would. Less deftly perhaps but crucially. Bogey just coz Alan Milburn looks like Paul McCartney. Campbells French polish. Overheads of plucking nits from the lady. Straight jacket or belong to Kirsty McColl. St Agnes Came to Skegness on a highness. Every year a birthday to you. Obedience own accurate figure. Divulge value of actual situation. Plane down circumstance. Ordinary complaint. Promiscuity causes resentment. High speed no maintenance. Moaning lot about handbags. Karen Millen shopping boutiques. Perfumery with wool and hair. Pluck on a stretcher for the the job situation. Palatable holiday deserve selfishness. Two hundred cost three hundred probably four. Cross pull over hand out. Clap of order. Bottom hoar and rise with a slap. Ten percent discount. Gym run the membership. Can't see everyday. Crop share whoopee. Blunder other culture me. On a mending spree. Punch is debonair with stalemate. Some tings are flu on the Salt n' pepper. Grandma pew smell worship. Stereo tonic. Bee kept suckle inebriate. Then George appears as a gorilla that Kennedy shot. Congregational mourning. Obsolete task enforcement. Free copy of a voice. Copy watch vice. Disdain a head of lice.

One party many in me. Plot wax toes. Wasp balm settle an old conclusion. Goodbye green celeriac. Treasure countenance They insist! Passport with a tongue to match. Moan in gangway. Fertile Proust read deconstruction. Couch says abused. Seep swab down. Mended spurn God bless you. A lot isn't acknowledged By laughter. Wheeze absolute by party. Serious interest stamp. Preservation order. Princes are coming. Croppings of loans. Gertrude bingeing smarties. Lights as guacamole if. Asparagus strawberry soup shake.

Coleslaw potatoes fetter cheese. Crisp enough watch Tracy Fountain in thirties black and white television. Work unison Page scone. Little clunk outside music. Martians under borrowing spells. Nightmares for twenty four shuttles. Biscuit earphone multiplex laser jet. Set twice for people who set examples. Thrice in urban planning. Criminals to those that can't stand them. Top and bottom example to some degree. Folk Robin, King Solomon, bird and fish, apprentice and master appetite in varied density. Correct path not investigated. Mindful extreme appropriate. Converge more common in theft. Clumsy chance need not pet. Correct exaction more than the answer. Work lift page reference. no proof of imprint in mental arithmetic. Multiply soul in addition.

M 2 x 2 = 2 in population single births A 2 + 2 = 4 M 2 x 20 = 500 or 20 A 2 + 20 = 22 or 22 is the difference. M 2 x 2000 = 200 A 2 + 200 = 202 The answer for 2 is 2 3 x 3 is not reproductive without DR

Father Son and Holy goat x Mother mother father.

There can be two doctored fathers. Technician team bring the game to rugby. 2 x 2 is dot cross dominoes Diane volume.

Weight Measurement wait in the emotional sense.

'Today baby it hurts that danger is pronounced in its descriptive form'. Long winded, a broken arm plays tennis years on. Sling from an arrow. Guilty arm assaulting and abating. Silent arm, bending to sobriety, rebellious one, cracking further up but never in the same place. Rings of innocence don't speak to the arm about the action. Natural pains are aging, bestowing grace on cat walkers. Danger happens and someone must describe the push. Some people get out of gardening through gates of slippery steps. Slippery people glean from the soles of their feet that cork can do grit wonders, just for treading on.

9
The Book of Zongs

This is a story about Charlie, which will astonish even the most boring people on earth. A long time ago in 1974 there was a pond in Essex. It was not very big, but it had a very special quality. The pond was the most beautiful mirror in the county. Birds from all around would fly over it to talk to the reflection because it was more truthful than any other pond in the region. It was a bit muddy on the bottom, a bit cloudy in the middle, and clear as crystal on the surface. Whosoever looked into this pond would always be told the truth. Some people would see how angry the clouds stormed, other people would see the patient stream, and some people could see nothing at all. All around were sky larks, bull rushes and ducks a dabbling for worms and creepy crawlies.

It was on the bank of this pond, which stood not far from her semi-detached house that Charlie's aunt would go and talk to the swallows and throw crumbs for any ducks that were hungry. The ancient proverb goes that it is vain to stare at your self in the reflection for beauty carries itself on the wind, in the wisps of willow trees, and on the sigh of falling leaves. In matters of discretion, it is always better to get a second opinion so that beauty can be heard in all things, whether they can be seen or not. Charlie's aunt was called Lucy. She never took any notice of what anybody else said, and the reason that she spent so much time on the bank of the pond was because she felt like an ugly duckling. All the ducks on the pond were preened, glossy and how happy they all were! The very sight of these ducks would cheer Lucy up. Lucy was sad because she was always losing things. When she was younger, she had always lost the other shoe, or she could not find her glasses when they were on her nose. But this time, it was far worse because she had lost something which just could not be replaced, although she could not think what it was. She may have been Charlie's aunt, but she was not his terrible aunt.

Charlie's aunt says she is alive and well.
She says she is a poor soul with nothing to sell.
It is wise not to listen to what Charlie's aunt says.
She is not alive and well
She is alive and terribly ill
She has been unkind her whole life
Charlie's aunt does not know
That I know that she is a
Liar, a thief, a beggar, a
beater, and a hater.
She has been mean and cruel
For absolutely yonks
For ages and for ever
absolutely non stop for
hours and days and days and
weeks and weeks of rubbish things on TV,
fortnights and years of nothing fun to do,
and for as much as
two and a half decades
decades
decades
dec..
Poor Charlie.
Charlie has had enough.
Charlie doesn't like names

Doesn't like houses
Doesn't like friends
Doesn't like jobs
Doesn't like anything at all.
Charlie is boring and shy
Sulky and cross
Stupid and dull
Fat and spotty
Lazy and selfish
Bored and rude.
Nobody likes Charlie
Everybody likes Charlie's aunt but it's not fair.

Far, far away at the other end of the country where people eat haggis and it rains all year, there was an enormous, gigantic, great big white house which stood in a majestic park a little bit smaller than Manchester. This is where Charlie's other aunt lived. The good thing about not telling you what Charlie's other aunt is called is because it is not fair on all the fairies and spell breakers who happen to have the same name as her. It is surprising that some people have names, when pigeons and swallows, worms and toadstools, cars and treetops often don't. Well, they may have a name in Latin, or a brand name, but not all of those are particularly special. It would have been much more useful if Charlie's aunt had been called a spare part for a Citroen ZX such as an exhaust pipe or even a steering wheel, although that would have been far too dangerous. She would have been more efficient as a BT extension lead, and more reliable as a rusty bicycle chain. On envelopes, she liked to be addressed as follows:

The MT Saucering Mrs. Caspar Jaspar
Twython-Mython-Swython-Log of Paradise Mansion
Heaven Knors
Carron Tweed
Fame

As you can see, it didn't fit on very well and so had to go on two lines. She was twice as angry when people thought that the second line was all the name of her house, although she never let it show. The reason for the title 'The MT Saucering' was that Caspar Jaspar's great uncle's first twin cousin twice removed had written a book about the day her mother had driven off in what was thought to be an MT Saucer from Nether Space Ship Yard and had never returned. Nobody believed it, but it was recognised as an astounding work of fiction. It was a best seller which made profits on average of around ten weather spells a minute.

The problem about that book was that although the story was brilliant far better than this one, it was obvious to anybody that in those days, 200 years ago, there wouldn't have BEEN a spaceship yard, never mind a Nether Spaceship Yard. Well I certainly didn't see it in The History of Onions or When Ghengis Khan Tripped Over. Even in exams there is no mention in of it in The Rise and Demise of Marks for Pences. But it was hiding. Even today, the North lands are jam packed full of aliens, the Middle lands are still popular as weekaday resorts, and the Southern seas are full of zongs, who are the more water-dream types of aliens. The real point is that aliens don't just fly. That would be far too risky, especially considering current levels of air streaks. But that is another story which we haven't caught up with yet.

Every time I think of Charlie's aunt, its nonsense. It would be more considerate to leave her out altogether. Charlie agrees. The only worry is that everybody must be forewarned in case they catch the disease of ever meeting her.

Her eyes on lies with spies are torn
The air she heaves is worse than bad egg droppings
She says 'Hiya' with dribbling orange tooth

And longs to taste what's freshly dead and dark

I know it doesn't rhyme, but she's too gross to make sense of harmony. But the catch is that SOME WOULD NEVER KNOW because she seems like a lot of ordinary, kind people who are quite nice.

1) She says 'As I was saying', and 'rully sad' and 'such a bore'
2) She still lives in a nice house in the beautiful countryside.
3)When she goes shopping, she smiles at people
4)She is bad at fishing

She practices showing her teeth in front of the mirror. For example, when she has just done something completely monstrous she will make her getaway by looking like she is very cold she thinks it is a smile and waving as she goes past, H E-LLO! and YIP-PEE. She might even try to wink at you, although watch out because that signals a worse crime. What I am trying to tell you is that her favourite occupations are baby eating, child snatching, skin baking and man chopping. I am the bearer of unbelievable news. Human eyeballs are her favourite food. They are one thing she really enjoys. However, since I do not want you end up in her larder, I shall pretend to the publisher that this is just a story. Oh dear, this is no good. Where are the zongs?

Zong HQ is located in the core of the earth. The oldest zongs live in rocks, and it is their job to hold the world together to stop it falling into space. All zongs are singing zongs. They are of the rainbow. They love salt in earth and solid stone. They shape the dew drop and ask the new born of sounds to sing to clasp to rock. Here is what a zong can look like

Most of them are temperamental and don't like to be disturbed by things with angry brains since they prefer cordiality. They are even more intelligent than Members of Parliament, but they find pollution and Hoovers especially frightening.

The reason zongs are so intelligent is that zongs spend their zonghood taking in brain messages and kindness. Favourite foods depend on where they happen to be and who they live on, but when in Norfolk, they do like lettuce. In Kuala Lumpa it is tropical bananas. All zongs begin as strands of hair. You may think that your hair is no good, and that it is just dead stuff which needs washing, but actually it is where all thoughts are stored.

It does not matter how many zongs there are, because one zong is as powerful as a thousand zongs. Zongs keep an eye on everything in existence, and have been growing ever since God began time. There are various types of zongs as you can imagine. There are head zongs, cheek bone zongs, wrist zongs, nether region zongs, big toe zongs, dog ear zongs, spider leg zongs, cat paw zongs, pony tail zongs, ferret knee zongs, pigeon toe zongs, and even dinasaur eye lash zongs, mostly rock zongs. When the wind blows, there are zongs floating in the air, when the stream rushes, there are zongs in rock pools. There is a zong for every star in space, and that's a fact.

Their journeys are so complex that it is silly for me to try and explain what happens to each and every zong as it changes. Long hair zongs have gained a bad reputation for blocking up sinks, and clogging up hoovers, for being in knots, getting in the way and not looking fashionable. It's all unfair because they are actually wilder than glory.

Perhaps I can explain it like this: When a cat nose zong blows off, say as it crosses a busy main road, it may end up in a nearby gutter. It could stay on the kerb stone for a moment before being whisked up in a breeze, getting caught in a twig. On that twig, there may be a hungry earwig who might nibble at it. There are lots of dreams in a mouthful of zong. Some things grow zongs, and other things eat zongs, but you shouldn't eat zongs if you grow them, or grow them if you eat them. If it doesn't get eaten it might crumble into earth dust, in which case it could float south to the Sahara Desert. Ten thousand years later, it could be rock, it might then be quarried, and end up as a fire place from where it could guage fire thoughts.

Zong that is eaten by slugs or wibs Charlie's aunt calls them bacteria, becomes an idea zong. An idea zong can fall into a line of ink, remind Einstein of a theory, or spark off a poem for Shakespeare one Wednesday afternoon. Whatever a Zong is, it tends to appear as a line. Michaelangelo Zongs are hung in museums because his turned into naked saints.

The room with flies
Is full of eyes
The afternoon man sits.
He scratches
And with a sigh
Picks up the phone
For a post competition
Free inhibition
Clip ties on paper screen
Wall chart on overview
Temps to divert for more
Custard in Germany
Bill sheets
And work plates
Forty seven ink jets
Maelstroms of harbour steel
Four million minds for meal
People to promote
Stations to save
Five bores to pigeon

A conference with tables
Maeve's birthday
And all before
Next Monday
When
The air changes colour
From gold to black and white
The liquid pen dries at the stem..
It is just

An aunt attack.

~

There has been some kind of dreadful interference from the thought of Charlie's aunt. Apologise for the enormous PAGE BREAK. The excitement of this chapter has all been lost, the afternoon man has disappeared and nobody can remember what happened because nobody else was there. In fact, the entire future has been lost. This book has momentarily lost the plot. If you want to help, one thing to do is to turn back to the last page and draw all over it.

The Missing Half has got to be somewhere.
The zongs know which means that you know.
Perhaps a password might help.

HOOWERYOO WARARYOO
ELEPHANT CROW
WALLABADOO WALLABADO

We cannot carry on until the afternoon man comes back.

This is ridiculous. All computers have floppy discs, disc drives, modems, ROMs, RAMs, screens, keys, buttons, arrows, blobs, letters, small, large and intermediate, or a PC to replace it.

In order to continue, go for a river walk to find some imagination.

NO SUCH THING. Is a favourite place which belongs to nobody everybody, including you.

The World

The only thing that the afternoon man left behind was the following note:

Where dead men lie there is a sky full of dreams, to stand is to see another. Gravity is the only place called home. Messengers know that words travel without guidance. Sound is a laughing rose. Tidy up the leaves for the worms in compost. The gardening twit sows rows of lettuces and slugs together. The tree is fly blown with caterpillars. Tomorrow's illusion feeds yesterday. The lab is an aeroplane, the bomb is a bus stop. The oozing waste holds appetite for nothing. Creep away on slime before time. Carry more sobs for the library store. Explain the dew drop where it rains all day. Fix an earthquake where there is no rupture. A wombling path is a shadow of pasture. The concrete morning of subways. All that is remembered was a hopeful star. The nest is in grasses on water, always there.

It is possible to follow the afternoon man. He shall have to return of his own accord, that is if he knows where to go. Losing direction can be a relief until you realise that you have lost what is choice. The zongs are reluctant to remind a man who has lost joy because lost people feed off sapped emotion. To become alone is to realise that what you are is not there. In such cases, the zong can only reflect an opinion held by others. If other people know what you are then it is a gamble to believe them.

TO RUST
Is a junk yard
For repair
Beyond the dump
For trampling relief
There is a paradise of warbles
Pile of marbles
And a jacket
Of mercy
Trust is good to touch.

This is a place which is ignored as senseless. There is no sense in deposition unless it can be retrieved. The pile above grows higher every day, the only escape is time. The rock will be good and strong in a million years. The packet fossil remembers a Wednesday lunch time. Tuna sweet corn mayo with iceberg lettuce still longs to be a BLT. It is an example of purpose remembered. It is freedom denied. Does anybody want to retrieve something with contents best before. Imagination is the recipe for depravity because this place is real. Imagination must not be a deferred vision of interiors and souls where all walk free. Imagination ignores the dump which is the store of creation because it is the dump and so cannot see purpose as viable.

THE GRiM HARPOON
Is not a pink Chapter

The battle of snow is a monstrous blizzard in which Druff tactics operate. The fight is a constant snort. For example, two years ago some especially rare Zongs of infinite capacity were captured in a GRiM HARPOON which Charlie's Aunt planted in the ladies room of a Gentleman's club. Zong snapping is a druff method of recruitment insulting. This is how Charlie became the afternoon man.

The rest is a bit too tangled to explain.

ZONGS ARE ZONGS ARE ZONGS ARE ZONGS ARE

Boomerangs.

10

Launderette, Tuesday, blue car. Steps washing pets. Who are the frumps, grits. Lump seducing disapproval.
Dear whore love gutted.
Dear You
Perception will clear with hard bench entertainment. Summarise flute inherited. Existence from mystery, new burglary. Premise of incubation, lower inflation. Taylor coffee shelf social stealth. Watch it brew. Tell on you. Who are the run of the mill. Peach political thrill. Why do cunts use the street. Good place pass to meet. Why do cunts overtake. Be obviously set apart. Brother chip shop three doors down. Head in a hairband. Brother small bundled plover, interesting days gawping at passing trays. Girl under her nose to defiant blue car parking. Just witnessed her future in vanity history. Slut no knicker, phrase deep wicker. Tenuous link fur ball, girl weave shawl. Happens nowhere else to park. Happens tails bring coincidence. Happens that gravy floats for handy frills. Incubator prove chalice on improvement, learn class self install. Large appropriation doesn't need to be on the run. Familiar install cue, married to be used. Pig tails not entrails. Valuable as specially treated leather. Process that madam likes, much as wearing tights. Careless writhe content in the afternoon, morning any tune. High street influence younger fleet. Complaint encourage unbroken tragedies. Entice beneath shop shed. Keep a prisoner in tell off. Citizens advice

educates. Forgetful to negotiate. Arrogance dismiss the under lords, right peep hole. Glitter inappropriate day, best served as obvious gravy. Chip send answers in struggle. Freedom to abuse is yesterdays muddle. All that carry on for thirteen year olds. Move out pre nuptial. Concentrate on gate, wary make compliance social reliance. Phones are human brands, consider coffee wanded hands. Growers of fine produce expect customer reputation. Apparently, with regards to family, union disbands by a third company unless the donor is internal, and relative to a flesh transfusion. Apparently the holy sensitivity on the ring is warped by outside. Neighbours looking in and out. The only answer is to mule the duff relation. Apparently the duff one is compliant reliant. Apparently begging emotion seals onward reels, untoward is positively selected. Retired shire soon to be on fire, young as she is. Apparently world predominance is the single solar plexus. Apparently coercion is welded on religious turmoil. Not all individuals are nuns as wayward turns. Yes presenting couples. Glory clean saddle. Round the course, something for Darcy. Literate to passing fancy. At the counter where the best book shines, fancies without strings. Stoics embed jewels can pray. Stoics have sheds with tools, sets with pieces of chess, collect doings as singles collect objects. change with chess lives. Brussel sprouts should be cooked nightly or early morning, they're also sheep's testicles. According to stoic yawn has no sense of dawning. abide the ways of stoic, is heroic. responsibility is invisibility, knows right. Careless plight knight, lance by marriage, pointing babies. Lean on nothing to give but receiving. Turn receive, died like mowing the lawn. Point a crop, turn too lush, needs thwarting. Enjoy good thrash. Physical options present hellos in salad concoctions. Refrains company and gorges. Chattering hallways in the absolute sense of inference. Grievance with constant nuclear threat, parallel strive. Used to be marriages of partners with brothers over there. Kid swapped or summer shopped; boarded for opt. removal from sight raises age where it might. Aunt dangerous, eight year old is more courageous. Existence draft on prior allegiance, inhabit social with family rivalry. Dynasty subsidy, too many cousins in mafia. Pig tail grafted to a quiet verge, rather like absconsion from a relative purge. Pig tail is not extraordinary, she is extraordinary. Extraordinary own fault. Prize snatch at village fete, although. Rampage hush at certain point. reigned in like bolting horse. Ghengis town and blether. Elvis blether with pelvis, song with spear. When Ghenghis prove interest, lay back and yearn or get fighting. Elvis deprived in front rooms, forgiven in spoons. Advantage on both men and masks as a shadow for a pen. Donor retrieve life between drip, hardly at distance. Bottle bank fridge but people directly. Cut swab thrown in bin. Injection lazer. Main recruitment of accident, careless. Turner expects to be paid delayed, no backing. Entourage far and wide at furthest expectation. mob not expect same flu. Decide to show up, fresh hand. Mob sowed near mould, slight resentment. Crowned makes room for one more. Listen singer baby. Chance invasion lets scandal subside by throng and beside. last time, not looking for Gavin. Carpet belong had influence as a courting child. Attention by dividends on blossom . Powerful in the duke of Westminster, possessed naked room. Encounter at the end of a buffer zone, wonders home. When did turn go home, and what was the outcome. Turn derive get, come, go and back again. Little impetus with forgetful, despite a brisk walk. Scenery owns a landmark, park tree waits. Expect hand and foot, passing breeze. Mark of significance, floodlight gives turn a shadow, special holly wood. Misfortune of shadowless talk is task. Step with typo blame, finger pressed there. Get off sentence if scoundrel in confidence. Turn lifting with what's around; board game to landing bound. insistence that monopoly knows sheds pound where a weight watcher perches. Human beings require bodily leanings, and combinations are helpful. When turn drops a stitch, best advance for builder's hitch.

Bulldoze makes car parks semi periodic. space is hatched correctly and office space more than likely. When vacuum is nationally secure, fortress manure.

Max has a seal of disable. Superhuman invitation sort confusion. Max could be elected or injected, people love him. bound to have leadership, poster board eating a chip. Has legs in plaster, he could run faster Max nods correctly down Mama Mia, looks like headroom. No obvious space fractures a pretty face, though it says go away. Doesn't live up to god's best way, starts boasting. Gets taken down from posting, he's tripped from the paper round. Could make a comeback if he hadn't been sentenced. Relents he is stud, still value in chewing the cud. settles for cheesy Watsits on his own terms. nice to pat. Max is she, lost his he, Max goes vegetarian. Likes to absorb ground from his spiral on the bottle pond. Sell milkshakes to the milky bar kid. is told to appreciate what comes and goes was gene's do. nothing without elevation, listen lesson station. Max doesn't like to admit that his granny was most of it, Mama Mia! gets fuzzed up to soften the blow of lessons. Completely overwrite him . When he was fine, he was wrongly commended for fraud. How were backers to know what Max would do, better risk in life on glue. Backers glue where they don't vote. Max did that, quote unquote. Backers are often invisible planners, sophisticate to urban wonders. What's the best deal. Mob save rubbish for Max's arrival, there's an awful stink. Realise after cognition, frosty morning. Becomes dependent with commuters pulling on choke, needs boiling in a kettle. One day Max will pull through. has much to do in far away environs. Lodged with paralysis, almost entertainment. If the mob would consider generosity, it would have the sun's shadow. Makes do with Watt not. begrudging explanation with wonderful laces. Max grounded with Laurel and hardy, Mardi foie gras. gets out of boasting about the sperm count, max won't head on. Max trouble with tongue, rent off glory.

pun sincere virtue. Max could recover the truth if leaking was Goofy. Goofy runs no time for words. Talks fast about counterfeit, knows full well. On the basis of knowledge max eats porridge. soak overnight consumed. Instructions for liberties. Bad men want Max's stetson. policies want Corpus Christi pun. Perched on a cloud where he was loud, blessings rained down. choice sprinkle could be winkle. Hands out watering cans, telephones. wanderers have mobile homes. Ingenious ways of passing. gypsy as epilepsy, he's an all rounder. Prank of letting off make do with fulfilling jaw trough. Captivity raise proclivity to alarming level. Max is Casterbridge seam, tidal as the river. max has places to dream that he could be marketing. Endows meadow as place time sleep. Balances positives on hot metal to keep them warm. Raids union flag to get well read. jumps ship at the same hip. Knows the passenger gang plank. push shove yank, lucky escape. operate minor confusion, turn gas backwards, bear left, step back, most adjective. Max formerly mentioned bankrupt. turned to Lowestoft. Has no cheese in his cud, eats silage. Isn't a cow for metaphor. Reinforces what heard with would. Lumps of wax for a hive that he scraped for ogre, feed ogre only relative. Believes health is white as a sheet. Plays cat's cradle. Answer when disproved, otherwise removed. Pelt navigate reach playing on beach. coast boat sure, now nothing done. Coast glass on table run, wipe the quickness polish more. Path of wander back again. OK demonstrate high failure rate. Blessed with unseen vest, could be a witty script. Knew martyrdom when his vest dangled. Gypsy word goes mangled. Stretches for his castaway eating kipper. Neither yum nor chum, television. Answers under duress, wants to join the police force. Max unclear about positive cheer that happened. Yesterday explained. Unusual take compliments from old dame. Wrestles fulfil word, tortured by the promise heard. Max promised he would provide himself a job, not be come an accountant. Learns the hard way that blank face sends up spray. Ignorance is opportunity times delay. Although the urge to talk is strong, breakdown awkward and long. finds churning out short of job. Has a bob. Would like to type letters. Feels sprung by dream, everything else lean. talk show last to know. Tells himself pitied for stealth, max knows the truth will out. When can he shout. Thinks shouting is dream demanding, car breakdowns Inverkiething. Terrible daylocked up by artful rose. Dodger thought lodger. gets along with lodger, plain biscuit. Thinks lodger wouldn't risk it, settle in. use TV as wing mirror, time behind flier. Has no anticipation of a buyer. Max between roundabout and Neasden, pedals alternate indicate. Daily motored, Max photographed. morph words that leave insinuate, Max spreads tar. persecuted by the trail of car, wafting an excursive exhaust. suspends tights with strangling. Friend suspend ham with jam slam. Suspends grief on a coral reef. Talk about headlines in spares. Art of literate opiate. Richness swap penicillin. tincture prove misadventure. Gallant to pink sweat. Put on a bet, gave charity some of it. Made gallant real come true and didn't give a hoot. finds donation with sleaze, night around day tickle freeze. Go between head and executioner. When greasy herring snoops round, it says 'why so long'. Picks week later sort charter, roll and thong. Wouldn't roll and thong but closest headroom. Max deliberates with horse tune, fit greasy herring both healthy food and sordid. Equalises satisfaction herring is right, cold as interbred makes white. Verse with prejudice, internal stack. Predominantly own fault at the expense of higher vault. Max rewards blessing with raw confessing. wonderful time steeped in growing a vine, hand rail engraved. max confide snoop and troop stalk would she were girlie. Max wants to pay income tax proportionately and isn't able to let them get on with it. won't infiltrate too late, needs to be collected. challenge to arrive, cannot go and liken skive. max adorns resentment with repenting, made up word. Callous wants to tell someone. Bolted without a blacksmith polish. Regard furnace to tend, room an orange blend. Stupid molten farrier. Prefers strangulation invitation to true adoration, slip flit of stay and sit, mainly pritt. Keeps majesty with travesty, door slits and skirt fit to impede movement. Pretend about improvement by talking about menus afterwards. Doesn't remember. Fix determination on this. Remember if the chance came, left in a hurry. Max wants to figure and fix the space, creates indent. Goes and assists the spiritually blind. Welcomes burglar deter and slur. Advertise sliding pun. Next best thing hairy nun. Schedule of drawing oaring. sees Argonauts in rosemary, read thyme. Breaks through tied with string, gets together with beat and bring. Functions best at strange limits and then becomes futile with blob and sky canal. Comrade on the radio, him. Mind a challenge screw existence. Political relevance imply exchange to chicken dual. Lay field sweat, catch of survival. verything talk on living extremity. Multiple coincidence threaten raft, number inclusive staff. multiple coincidence threaten happiness, all jump on. Would have thought code alarmed happiness. When money explains warm socks, socks in the shops. Money no longer important. Grits can appreciate the zest of deodorant, bed sheet stresses take actual turns. Cast iron constitution imbued with south westerly pees, folklore right wing cheese. Confess best million, represent last dragon. Precede unprecedented, something unusual in safeguard. writ ahead of schedule, vegetable delivery. Max saw life in worst case strife, alleviate. imagine if threw gif. invent marketplace demand. state of delusion go round Waitrose, disappoint trap. Mungo squabble beyond, curse dextrous to clash and pause. Those two go round together like a mountain sherpa. Hurried crash of anchovy, sign off desertion, shopper scarper. Man by sprouts isn't openly hostile. Friendly Shane tried to sort waitrose, mungo means potatoes. Albino olive and pancetta share college, what course is that. 11th Feb. hard to understand a death swap. confiscate son because she orally killed hers. Law upholds to the state that is. Several case exonerate by luck. There's a kind lady waiting outside. Bride escapes the altar situation. Child cries, sure isn't sure. Thank you thinks she's grateful. Says she says. Thinks the crime illustrates. Farts on cue, laughs like one that's due. Show card, there to explain. Unwraps for what she goes through. Partial to painting. Learns when the rules are absurd, gas strikes home at the edge of the world. Air free standing, cause to resent. When woman flowers in the attic, ballistic likes to extrapolate. Kinky fun with take on dead baby's gum. stands to act snipped to enhance the inward stripe. Woman from prison thinks there's nothing wrong with lederhosen. Woman from prison brushes ponies with a dandy brush. Flowers don't live in the attic, they might salivate. Things that make him say yes, yes. Salute the woman in the prison from the prison. Pay attention to the romance of what the woman prison wants, puts head in. Collect desperate exile with clouded dream. Blank boy with the go go sister, got long hair. Mildly jealous of seven year old with guitar on a strap rap. to the drinks party dressed au pair, pass boy but not on the stair. problem upstairs, baby in cot, many years ago, problem hope left. Problem solve, ready steady revolve. Panics a bit and retreats, yes prison woman higher than peak. Thinks climbing a high one is the best answer to maybe. Delaying a good word for postponing. Delay what happens to the woman in the prison. Woman implements delays on the run, accelerates on vehicle that gasses. Ga ga kiddie wink, counters on table stink. Likes bungee jumping. Apparently the way to know a stunt. Stunts every now and then, has a tumor. Watches the telly, has TB. Doesn't mind until what she's looking at. Doesn't look at anything properly. Wonders if Loona's dad is Aboo. ABOO Loona called Diana and Bionic. thinks about things and does sod all. Situation set stale cement. sits in London, will repent. Thinks the strategic way to solve is problems. Gee could very strong. Time has passed and moved. Boy thinks home a tad unfair, thinks his mum's a murderer. There. Might not think that he might have to contemplate. daily spat proximity of what's next door same room. Easy to remove its flaw. When Bin laden lives upstairs there's a joke to pay in bus fares. thinks of novel solutions to social permutations. cannot abide the idea of Noel Edmunds. Looks trouble in the eye and says fuck the news. Actress, goes through corners then ignores. carries on proud to be in jaws. Quite a sight to watch, isn't she. recedes like film titles. Something she did earlier. Goes on a walk through the woods. Beating adventure. imagines she's holed up on hollywood, too right. Thinks these things and more, confides in what's around her, just a claw. gets away into thinking she's pulled something off. Trip to a hay feeder, sits on top. Glad nourishment for the spiritually flawed, good to eat. Pig can't control her appetite for shortbread. wolf fingers, triangles and circles on the same day as porridge and haze. Neighbour come back for more. Used to own her own private train, what a sentence! Press two three times instead of one, should the exclamation. Puzzled by reality, funny how it bites. Needs lights to understand what could be feasible. Goes to cinema not in tights. Run out of tights won't crap. Doesn't have any pants. Wants service secret and stretch around sky. Disassociates toiletry folklore with the means of dogs and horses. Mucking out is private for humans. Different things all the time, walks many lines. Expects to be invaded by those who think she is chocolate flavoured. thinks she is chocolate. Crisps think they're fish n chips and barbecue beef. Wonders what is officially thought, bought up not brought up. Main reason for living in catch up. Visitors arrive to cracking noise, floorboards awkwardly as toys. doesn't make that noise. Shouldn't really be here, place grubby colour. embarrassment about smell choking. Visitors dive into the bathroom, bin is honking. Could have put the rubbish out, thinks didn't want to. Small and want smell. Stink doesn't, thinks metaphor. Quite proud of smell in some ways, just isn't sure when to clean. Hears smells, forgives. Nutter has a laugh. phrase at the edge of slide are ridiculous. Woe betide at the end of the buffer zone. Stop sign thanks. Wanted to be asked to parties, who take. Wanted to be arty fartie. Went along with the idea of dropping a boy off with his sister. Knew boy was blister, did she. Said straight he'd copped something larger than fate. Thought she'd get found out if she went and lived on spaghetti. Thought she'd be found out if she'd bred with opportunity. In order to prove a point. Left the boy without immunity. Thought she heard a crack at the door and jumped up. There's a flaw. Thinks she's a religious extremist, can be good at tennis. Thinks she wants to play ball with dogs, thinks cleverness lies with hogs. Thinks she's Danish today, yesterday a pope's display. Relativism the box is in, ties of knots with string. Could say that and get away with it. presented with four ingredients, ins, outs and disobedience. knows disobedience is best revolting. Thinks point of suitor is coyote boating. Extent of odd occupation marvelous to circus nation. Keeps saying she'll come round to acrobat. clause walked wire, knows her thinks. Needs bad people to keep mad, calm and pliant when she isn't had. Wants to tune into the radio at the right time but wants to miss out Noel because this is his line. Got worked up about courted. Noel is a horse in some respects. Sirius and circus are closely linked. Stars beyond the sink. Mary's sauce has got something to do with a trench, though it has lemon and thyme. Computer switched off during the bath run, this could be explained. Ronnie Courbet sorbet. The day is deeply unsatisfied. Worries about the paparazzi, paparazzi was. Thinks Ian would have called if she hadn't eaten the sauce. Eats me sauce with cabbage and drops. leaf by the drop off bin. Gets fluent with confession, lumps and bumps easy with prospect. Audience thinks of Lemon tree fiasco and very annoyed about farting on the dictionary, still an extremist. Couldn't get past a canon lens if she wanted, no e. Thinks Jamie Oliver's sauce is like Terry's force. Thinks right after a solemn pledge not to, then buys it. hollandaise for summer, wants a friend like tom that she locked out when it was not warm. Kind of remembers to her own detriment. When dead leaves have gone under. Late to open. secret admirers when she lets on. Called Ian and Tom and all the leading men. Likes leading men, good for role development. Would like to have access to a bakery, still isn't welcome in the supermarket. Got shopping list of perfect proportions to probably. £66.8 at 7.15pm and good misunderstood. Yin yang numbers corrected by the disk utility on the mac drive. Thirty three better. Got 33 in her organic delivery unintentionally. Thinks number in Wilde film says 33 for prisoners. But that prisoner that shouldn't be there. Interest assort spelling mistake. back said £66.9 at 08.15. Choice stay in on Saturday night. turn down a medium treat. go somewhere outside an office. weather cold and old. Press scales. most important thing.

Valentine's day in one solution. bear no conscience. envelope hug embrace. death stung nicely in a parcel. Christmas treat Dickens. Today is giving. Keep mental flaw guessing. Trick. Multiple personality bag time. Strict disapproval about the east. three o'clock at afternoon swine. Poor scale the hun must home remain. darkness is idle fame. All afternoon east, penises and idol worship, worse of than sneaks. All morning mourning, lazy from dawning. What's the energy. Americanisation uses affirmation. tongue telepathy the British scene. Abscond to Gatsby, truly terrible after style. at least there's a real life option. Fake pardon misinterpret by love. Let's use that. Fake pardon not inclined to know about death. Fake park don get reason. All day and all night troubles for September. Thirty one days that remember. When the time comes, wardrobe finishes. Breakfast coffee for tea. Backwards to the day, water is less charged. block reluctance worthy of penance. Character love seminars. Some ways forward see nothing but other people. All considerations done for virtue, stop the treacle.

Hey, treacle that's you. Treacle word up stick. November's Guy knows five's a height stupid. Gatsby enough dull to quit.

Butch rolled body, go eat a banana. Gatsby switches off, mysterious just disappear. sofa mild opportunity to reign in the clear. She's taken the wide berth of leaving scenes and looks again through the teleport. A Was Oz dream. sofa understand log out procedure, can just leave. Heroine leaves, and credit rolls. goofs troop out, supermarket. spelling flaws of what leaves are clues to men that like Jeeves. There are people who take instructions seriously about how to avoid death. there's a Marple on. Shouldn't be twitching but there is when attention must remain intact. Far usually flaws and bother. Tiny things remind heroine to remain where she is, getting good at blowing cover. used to do the Claridge set with cocktails. Had a slick informer and didn't have to choose for herself. problem with estranged solitude sticks around hollow good. Too much importance about doing anything. Constant supervision or direction. she cannot be true to her herself. Bad things to get in on how to feel. harsh tourism. Drinks at the pitted stall and takes self defense classes. In play within play, gets her way. gets to subside and exalt, says it's malt. Explanation pump out stories. some flicks are special effects. Most important thing is to wear slacks and then do seizure. Juggle humanity loves profanity, insanity, recovery. Swiss take Swedish baths, Norwegian tubs, whatever. Plunge and shine beautiful time, next test amnesia. Can the plan remember and kick. Suit college require knowledge. Voice must be found. Impressionists all round for being watched. May not proportion life to box dissident. Try take position, stick to wing if must. Fill in for injury, wants to buy and post at the same time. Visits the office in the afternoon, stands in sunshine. Claims faults in mud, glorious powder, workshop sud. Heroine Rose shed envy and no one knows. Went bright red when audience sped, got an oscar for it. Complaint heroine right sends into night night, type cast. Poor woman from following around tied to ship's mast. solution numbers on with selfish constitution, what is the point being separate. King

Kong puts his fur on. points at buildings like chip munks.
Relevance to disaster persuade look faster, woman tiny to
get. Giant coincidence of obtuse; ignorant tickle. cheek want
scratch nothing hatch. Speed coincidence. Chime needs. If
woman licks, she is infatuated. Proud to banish in charge of
e-fit. seventeen years old could be up or strung with the rest
of them. Apply comic and learn paraplegic, the two weave.
Talent argument sensitive concede. retort offend. All for
pretension. Height with building looks. However overhead.
precise connection complicated. Orb string woman's weight
with earth, she feels. Cannot undo she reels. man from casting
position. Unpleasant endurance makes moles of mountains.
This is how the lady feels. Compensate distress improve
behaviour, more technological these times. performance
achieve house, well matched silver. Pleasure silent, happy
furniture.
'There are so'
is the wrong phrase. This for threading air. Heroine fortress has
multiple particulars and may lose sight of her own. Just watch
affairs romp home. Particular stress on conservative press,
social chronological. Best invention apparently no tension.
point about wealth enjoyment. Go burger stall from an above
view, any disclosure. Judge achieve place by asking where to
face, questions for disobedience. Know all takes anything
pleasing. Poor heroine still can't wrap a shawl, likes to be
haunted with vested interest. Complication attention. things
trend near invention. won't hear of attention and invention, she
is genuine. marketed when pearls landed round her neck. wore
glory above anything she could express. Swept away, film
effects. Path to follow secure, subject of placing bets. Call
woman fault, wrench soul. Tidy bar perfect tunes, match visitor
install. When heroine falls she musically stalls, her company is
time to pervy waste. Marks the foot unchaste and watches how
to measure it. At three at four, scrambles for stripping reason to
the jaw. If heroine could manage to narrate her curiosity she

would become out side with philosophy. Would like to teach the world to sing, oh yeah. Things she didn't mean. She will want. she has nothing, wants to prove her point. Finish potato, will buy an envelope. Will question the purpose of hemp oil. surface hair only head gear. Touches back of neck, scratch tickle enough. Gracious oration isn't busy enough to tell her punch line. Obscure face from daily trace, no less complicated. tries to stay in bed, not lifting a finger. Fail movement pace of eyeball lace, sift dirt. In films there's an expression, gone this morning. Flick dirt in the face through dust in the face, that was it. Misspells Eeyore, clever. Does flip charts like men's press ups. won't be allowed again. Sun takes an awfully long time to set, lights can't go on yet. Muses on injustices, finds martyrdom. Had three months of Bahamas and had luxury pajamas. Threw problem in dust bowl and called fatigue. Positive mormons don't like to be undermined. value of search not left behind. How long does heroine have to live. What point of panic for pea in sieve. wanted to know what happened in the film, hadn't seen it. Seen it only when she wanted it. Unable to recall what she wanted when she gave. Has no wants when she is found, love all around. laughs the subplot. Has to wash her hands when something lands, gets found out and question to boot. all body and wisp, strength in mannerism. Bout of anger set in, action colloquial. Bout of hopelessness sets in, black and white to dub sound. Can rearrange profound, pressing buttons. Solution of restrain tells name to get back to jam, is the farm. When rescue operation comes, purpose for harvest. Anything solves collected by trolls, harness meaning of life. What is heroine going to say next that isn't seduction's day. wants sustained mall of glories call, wants permanent address. last film was queer fiasco, needs to bat and ball. Twenty three parlez vous, mostly overwritten. Presses scales, patchwork shale and beach is long. Where is heroine going. Tries to worry about having existed. Tries to prove that she is by going on line. Acutely good at doing undo, makes improvements on backward journeys. Thinks system doesn't recognise her apart from dreamily, how soon till death. Denies death most seconds, she says she isn't in yet. Always maintains she isn't by what she can get. Looks at the word, oxygen and drugs, says things she's never heard, isn't true. Heard would on the ground with her ear, Indian sent whoops. Mangles her problems with multiple solutions she could hold spear if she wasn't sick. eats couscous and gooseberries for sweet and sour, wants honour. Had honour this morning for a short time but turned her back on Gatsby to eat lunch. Sit through the entire production because didn't think. Should be doing reflection, wants ink. Has nobbled throat, thought bulb would fix her quote. Bulb is only part of the story. Illuminator to wayward inches too dim. Bulb is hyacinth bouquet to neighbourhood swing. Does one thing and demands ovation. advertises snacks, watches the phone ring. Applies what she must avoid to things for carrying. Did go through her own fault. knows how to run round the track in the wrong direction. Thinks she could swerve to enhance this fact, what else could she do. Could slip round the back of nothing else, try when busy. more tired because of radiotherapy, when illness becomes. circumspect sets in, appalled by secondary treatment, has advantages for the wrong reasons. Heroine wants toughest subjection to apply adversary, oh no she doesn't. sees hop ops and thinks of coughs. was that the child she bonded with, was that confiscation. Would know her mother if she could account for addition. Waits to watch the television, what's the gap. Waits to hear the radio, usual rap. should not listen to the radio, is a goldfish. Has been dunked and rinsed tomorrowish. Tomorrow comes for her, knew ago. Treatments for the slippery. Home for the worrier. will find the cause of brain damage to be an illness to manage, will receive no compensation nor explanation, will reap hurt in slings. Broken arms of dusting will resort to dusting. That says dusting. will go round and round in the minds of dervish, didn't want Dante to mean anything. Now what, says heroine, slang for swearing. Cannot say a word without some definition of cursing. time delayed for what she portrays, only pursing and the money is running out. page fifteen again, close to the reminder of most useless ploy. Hand notes to several quotes, intellectuals raise hopes but drew them in. Needed revolution. o a long day. boy of expert joy hides from clobber. Bob a frightening name, game and close vowel ears, laugh Black. bladder jowls, knows Silesia. head half removed, switch by rude. think stays, stile plays. Hear on string sings. Voice distant man, wants choice. Cares tell lies, body always stronger. Winnings, bets, dares. wonders for edit sprout fears. says Bob does. Should put on gloves. Remove statute still rescue. Although bob is fifty percent, world flat for upside down. thinks bars pearly highs, chances reinstate gigantic ties. Tie tops underneath, ribbon scrunches crinkle. shape of Bob's ear could be interesting, accommodates finger. Believes in true extension, fingers blind invention. could know what Bob did by alarm. Most hid in the outbreak, action take. Ear formulaic to language, thus instruction sandwich. Approves promise for hope, ear scan eye scope. Senses genesis, box tennises. enough stimulants to keep busy until home time. Half divine for extending lead, watch that go away speed. Arrives okay, what happens with go away. Clings to sweats and stings, needs paralysis. exhausts the state of repair, gets exhausted. could be more exalted if lessons were strong. Wants to pass no question. Keeps doubt stoke . Bound to get wet pants. Controls pop ears. Patrols pop tarts. Bob has sliding scales of dangerous ants, slip around. Artistry of humility smothers with pounds, floats on heroism sounds, squashing prior convictions. Honoured with predictions, bob's angle unusual satisfactions. Bob may know about that because of the level of fat. Bob may bounce up where the rest crop. Bob would like to observe what to conserve, only way up. Pit belong donation foreign station. has hair on her shins implanted, hair from reunited. Solution in the end silly joke, pull off the plug hole, choke a teenage curl. Sort blink from pauper to earl. refers she's Bob. Plug just promotion. Horse cob and corn share dinner. power on blink. flutter eyelash, tease sacrifice. Two where one will do, isn't crying visual drops. 15 insults beyond intention, ready kindergarten. Dines above the old school, lizard spit strongest rule. waiter stupid too clever, comment makes a tether. Waiter says done, plastic waiter amenable fantastic. Thinks of all the speed in the building, black pots of paint and loud music. suggests jews are composed, says they are. concern for volume painting, great audience in waiting.

Frances can't remember of the name of Christopher Hitchens and Martin Amis again. Eats lunch without too much fuss, turns a room with no fuss. Commentates the likeness and gets out of it. The infringed are mildly haunted and amused. Squashes the posh, larger things. Ultimately richer without doubtful story rings. thinks she'd better overtake the curly haired girls with the reminder milkshake. was better than Laura, she was better than Claudia. Has been worrying strategically about the rally, cooks need to evacuate before lunch in the quad. Appears then dismisses her job, doesn't eat the first raspberry in the creme brûlée. Book says Razz-berry, she'd never have believed. insults without meaning leaning to. Feels ugly has a strange power in show. has no oil for words, hasn't spoken for weeks. Who's to blame if she can't say the right lane. doesn't think when exchanges she speaks, this is zombie-hood. Only half hears what she gets, mistaken her devil. Says what and learns from Neville. gets espresso for nothing, takes one sip and price is reducing. Would have liked the number to reach 27, isn't a truncheon, oh yes she is. Tries not to consider the attraction about what she'd say to the fashionable section. Ignores the older couple by preparing to leave their welcome in ways. Stirs insecurity from the paces she lays, doesn't expect her own comb. Goes straight home and says balls many times, wastes time with philosophical line, shouldn't have spoken. Street busier than musician stand, all scratch nits and point around. heralds exactly what she is, these words are her fames, sell them as she may. Types to illustrate warning hypes, thinks she's just got to rehearse to get it right, fuck first time, actually swears. Laden with illness and wetness, needs to shrug. stretches patience over the hanger sags. Francs are Romans. sums are hags. Amazed at what she learns by fudge. Thinks she'd concentrate more and get stuck, go with someone and wake up. does fine under the wing, goes to school on her own ring. Doesn't want to be defensive, can't know everybody and insulting is the best offensive. Doesn't does n' dry. Thinks random wheel, thinks attempt is common stealing. Doesn't want to pass tests, too high for simple jabs. Constantly entertains lost cause, round of applause. news break familiar and new. oh that's true. restaurant has friends. considered until the back view. Friends that were do well from nostalgia. fear is time advanced. Falsely precise. Dislike and sweet anxiety ring values forever. Was that going to be as instantaneous, is the best mistake obvious. According to norm, true north is close by. Even on change, the angle is apply. Needless to say dizzy hurtles from sickness, restlessness, district changes course election. Own back again glimpse one to ten, these friends are counters. When do the times shake the futures. Most seals are supposed to be takers, gifts of life among packing cases. Market shop parenthood for undermining what it wants. Lady has a shabby head, visiting early, lady has a rabid dog, scent to bite her. Like most tender gardener, irritate irk will call the name wrong. mrs to mrs not, switch night falls. Everyone is nervous about madam match, she deserves the odd latch. Cowers in terms of noting insult, glowers and relinquishes. Stakes are with interiors, flowers raise edible vegetables. Start gun bangs through cordial fizz. If the seminar burned truly, diplomacy washes. If the idiot prize is all that matters, eat candy floss. Point is that shoving works. Worst flaw is governed socks. Have pairs and crutches, bodily urges link keys and purges, watch them d@sh! Mysterious scouts are all surprise, boys must stick up. Mysterious with transformation, seller buyer eyes. When the bullet art does there is no proof like moving. month of February is bagged corn, autumn delivery. Lease expires gradually like cup broth, day by day. Outback is distance to far and away, same recipe outlasts. Accusation whose man knows more than accusation, another predatory situation only requiring flunky's word map. Flunky says Into trap. This was confirmed at lunch. Situation overcoat close to slump. It hangs, play retrieval to lateness, the stuff of danger to actors. Like cowboy factors, extractors. Life in vector exactors. Street cleaners go whirring at the port folio that nobody knows the ace plan; class. Fashion reflector is the word now. Say now for backward kowtow. Fashion reflector, justice selector, say No, say yes, answer make up. Can the voice know what it does to rubber face. Can the voice attend justice to lace. Without effort the dialgogue is invertebrate, film scored to standard snored, puppets to barbaric hoard. Value choose takes cheese upon, something Albion. Visitors have not been and gone, the awkward geek wonders from. Opinion demands dominion, the blank hurts. Most exalted pass is through to cornucopias. What like is to play mike, hear their own space to presentation. Visitors don't sit in darkened rooms waiting for the lights to change. Who lives at the space of continence, who does. Venn diagram does the hour later, expectation grit detection. The teas maid lays the tray and all the rest have their way. Step aside is information, kilter off is subjugation. Gardener rests with plants and nature, this has been business planned. What gardener catches does mice to people flan. The permanent excerptors hum their own tune. Wake the stubborn choice to the seminal ground, there are decorative weeds. Cultured area turns malaria, tunes. Face reports exact mistrust, bodies exhumed. Treat the case favour not oddly. Sharing switches just ungodly. When the visitors snoop, romp about. The instant of achievement, (visitors arrive). Purchasers won't when they're posh, take as tosh. Brazilian millionaire looks round the cube, gets ejected by the best if they do. The Brazilian millionaire would buy for someone else, something stored. has to apologise for answering indirectly, swallows on her own apparently. feels dizzy and wonders how long. Flat line pissing waits till nine fifteen. All that holding in. Time extension stretches rubber till the prize is only rubber. 16 knows john, a matter of life small J. reasons afterwards why she was angry. The post office makes Frances angry, her distributed soul. rounds that sentence off, cool. Gets not racist and impatient in the queue, also sexually confused. Is strung to the e-fit, shays she's strung. is the E-fit of what she opposes, she resolves she should know john. Will Frances recognise things before goodbyes to what she did wong? Collects would have to value going gone. could kill the existence of regret, it wouldn't let her pass. tried to do the post office with glamorous pass. Left her lights on, had an open boot, three dimension faults to what was at the root. persistence knotted on her face, fuck off smile, she has to . Thinks the Scots are out to get her, gets picked on. This is true like scratchy nits, should be thankful. After all this time the outburst is wronger than the actual crime. For all pity had an awful time, blew so strong she may have served time. does serve time. What does this mean. Death and the post are mean. All hot under the collar even with sedative dollar. Could watch morning television to counteract the cost. has clues all over glues, rips and pauses for dippy perfumes. When the woman with the same bag isn't actually black shack. plays in the way to snuff out her plaque. writes this, but the close match doesn't rhyme the ropes of dirt can catch her sign. More knows her path is bedfellows, jokes all day she is gay, really is. Rides the wind along the quiz, all trousers. Shouldn't be a problem, only suffocation. Death and creeps at the same station. Offend the genuine helpers. darts in fly backs. kind that pin down. stays to tacky perfections. Bottom fringes of suggestion, clearest profile. Bothered by a lesbian mile, isn't irony. Values delay, knows John knows Peter Kay. Programs remind to say. Does remember with a flaunt. How responsible is the feeling, can it install. Crap is valuable after a bar, dot dash dot Sunday spa. nothing to stop from slipping the habit. offensive. blame as a patient treat, wrong person in restraint. Person could there be the other, person nails animation. Little digit exact cue, attain understanding to the extent of what digit. pen draws. Says animation, means voodoo, odd word, odd distinct, odd separate, cartoon has no line without swerve. It means to be gay, dead is gay. Repercussion. Gay fury on the run. Wasn't isn't. Definitive that says being. Gay envelope tsars group. toilets at hour intervals, something like that. Famous hedgehogs cross but deers are volume terrors. Fury maintains more than queue. Times of anxious fighting. Settle the Viking scores. Present adopts to keep rights. Penance retorts, confession fluid. Age of reticence holding back. the sorry container. Hulk with green giant exposure. Loop custom for telephones, information. Reluctance to accept will not wear frills. close chance gets sent away. Can be funny to watch. there goes a wart hog. Convenience of something bigger hampered by spiritual flaw. Axe the guy to save the day. guy say girl no way. girl sap curl. Medallion sad stallion, world broccoli. Vegetable taste civilisation. Fought through. Last true to a thousand. Sit and knit. Ambidextrous style pit. Modest at that. Time for punch. Serve and whistles. key grab a barrow boy. almost approve. Dirt jockey part of the ploy. Meet the woman who sends back. Small went round the tree the wrong way. Bin man goes the wiggly way. Caught in the rain. oh this again. complexity of forgiveness. Badly needs the loo. Stale clove, broken off from yesterday. First person after third, present to be heard. Onto a winning streak. Hear Oasis play, blame them anyway. Almost starts all over again. nips through a down clown. back up tonight, TDK KT Tunstall. Fed up of funny romances, may have worked in the post office, has no record. Fidget quivers and stamps, runs, jitters, steps between. remembers people like Jill and MYOB. Less than a sign. intelligent enough to think time. Policing is stressful and indignant. Yes and no malignant. Chart about commitment. Foot cross weave exact loops. Nicely in a question mark. Retrace toe five a time. Signs of hidden intelligence. To Sir with Love. Life land. Stowing bandits like MYOB. first come, haranguing first served. On her wave of glee deflates like a balloon and has the excuse. That woman trapped me. MYOB is a situation, only activate personal. activate wrong equations; hers to solve. Uses schoolboy voice in the shop. Walks on top of where the woman came in, species woman. Fills in, just after the CD. Has no one to ring, thinks the tender is familiar. Doesn't raise her eyebrows that much, just a bit. Glad to get out of the shop, what was that. Finds the expedition smoother in the car, trip easier than bus by far. Thinks she could punt. Should mind that Fulham made its name from her. Why be anything but thankful to blanket stakes of reclamation. urged on Holland. collections up for grabs. Feats of engineering. The attentiveness of young men is nice. Answers pleading lice to complain. Lopsided wheel hasn't mentioned old portfolio. Dealing doesn't appreciate. Thinks miracles are what looks like. won't be allowed the satisfaction of selling the meagre plot. overdrawn has to borrow. The point is she could go tomorrow, instant death wish. can't stand the obstacle plant. veers without veering, independence back route. Streets emptier, re that sort of idea. would be emptier. daze of Oxford shopping, interpret slant. bother starts off from Centre Point. Nag letters on the step and washing problems, media coverage in the stuff of clanging dreams. point about what sounds nice. Better to wait in the smell of the food. Ravenous all day. Spent without a watch to match. twenty twos, fifty twos, thirty threes and sixteens. proper tables have seats for sixes, not ones and twos. clothes won't wash with polyester. Parp parp from place to road cross. Be matched to take a walk. Not really having done it. significance of inability. about avoiding. Part time sake, fifteen better than sixteen. Shoe lose a footing from sodding exaction. individual prospect for the escort of service. Pace a corner hatcher, all alone on a one leg gaiter. Lonely person doesn't want company. forms of understanding. First preventative. music be mistaken. no not that one. signify deprivation. Setting slightly crooked, omnipresence can't be helped. Craftsman perform, didn't have a bow. A hunger of now thinks staying in is to clean the scene. knows before doesn't do. entirely starving could like. Could have a filling benefit. Resolve and volume nearest to furthest. Greens brought from distant lands. non descript a baby language. Wonder of high street tans. contact next table. Mabel possession. Person object to being included. restaurant severely deluded. What would the choose like. What take direction. mid sentence no time to eat with a fork. Bread absolutely delicious for the face it makes. Nutty differently. taste the nut bread. Decorate it to a falafalish round thing. Finger food. Fork a ridiculous metal tool. Eat the triangle japatti. samosa something triangly. inbetweens. Restaurant deals chat with deliberate shits and telephones. Success cause consumer. Bess Tasted before. How did it go. Time and existence hard to bestow. why was the walk so easy. Drunk values aren't on the same permit. Olive back to leave a stone. Sober rule strongly defined. case of schizophrenia. Nose brush disturb a customer. constant acknowledgement furtive cluster. Friday project a problem for Frances. Thinks she has problems with you romances. Most convenient priced from tragedy. Sign very clear. Most clear, more understandable to everything. Child problems are definitive perversions. What can be said of returning from to die. answer back in Google humanely. Plate must finish a line of no limit. Ask if the restaurant is open.

draw attention. Look for the question of problem presentation. harmless rotten. Good documentary. Good biography, good extremity. insistence to eat chick peas. Play hard to please. indulge against forbidden bulge. Didn't know. wind slips, end passed. No allowance for eating fast, except too fast on television. Saturday of wall swabbing. Desires of red paint all over, flanked by beige and ribbons on the tables, just like weddings. Enough time passes. Olive have to be swallowed. enough time for people on their own. Ben and Jerry's ice cream an oscillatory mean. Joint eat the tub. Leave a single in the scrub. cushion benches for wenches. Woman in the ribbed polo neck wouldn't be given. Pair matched red. they're both in jumpers and dark trousers. Further away man looks like a friend. smiling at the distance of enjoying. When the attention has dinner, back out only slimmer. Fast behaviour is knowing what to say. World is on its way to not staring and making people feel gay. Gay is unmatched and matched in that order. When broadband is okay it has land dispatched. Connection means speed when net connectors only want a nice feed. telephone rings the glass and doesn't sound like it breaks. Music isn't boisterous. Last part of the sentence from the margin was filled in a Gucci fall. Mistake of someone else is universally significant. Could mean there are clues to notching up a work shop. Red jumper man knows clues and his past arms of good looks. People don't know what they can realise, but all know the life ties. Point about desperation is incapacitation. When blind dog comes home again he isn't able to bark. Dog could bark like sneezing. dropper has elastic on his shoe. Shows signature to girlfriend, probably nothing wrong with what he did. Girl confident enough to make him seem not much more important than her. Woman probably red jumpers' daughter, wife whatever. Twenty eight year old story subject has tantrums at her age, what's wrong with her. The resort to persevere with the bite of bread crunches the cheek, the sign of the week. restaurant is mainly about lamb.

£0.75, house speciality. Knits set into more break, the woman with red and black dangles suggest past quangos. pashmina woman has toys with friends in numbers. Volume increases, isn't one yet. Olive last prompts southern gases, red table smoke molasses. need to eat at table quasi fable, what should happen to leftovers, what should happen to . Man in the hat takes it off, disappointingly bald but with shaded glasses. Aren't many caricatures that dominate rooms, hatted and booted. only rhymed booted. One curlier hair than eyes, hair seen first. Equal talks through dinner, aluminium rudeness. Roots growing out on the way to the toilet. Food isn't enough, even making the booking. Standards about other people are knives and plates laying tables. Contexts and complications aren't supposed to be resolved apart form presidents. The way people suck their lips has nothing to do with hips. Aluminium keeps announcing that bread gets delivered. Launch a desert is marginal to time's perch, how long can the sitter protect the rooms interest. the gut has already expelled behaviour's part, man pinches his nose. Table cloth has sauce and crumbs, rose gone back to. Face press legs cook where pudding plods a lonely mule. Lonely being observed in the lateral tense of served. Lonely mule designed to bray with cleverness. Co exaction of doing is clever in its own way, couples and mixed groups tables are doing more than stay. Mule proves the point that seating is for one point. Point about tantrum most interesting, the whole nightmare is not worth suggestion. Someone saw the popcorn flaw about Elm Street, the big issue of saw beat. Channel switch is easy switch, at least alternate. Say pitch. There was hardly anything left on the plate, there was hardly anything. What might happen at home happens on set, there's no problem with faraway get. Did that get that problem, did that set that effect, did that present a larger and rounder fret. If the words are just exploded, future hangs raw, if words are future sounded, remembered. Channel honesty to travesty demands audience attention, certificate to mention.

What seen is presented green, stile the prejudice. Be appalled, dismiss and be stalled, say back to Baclava, say filter to coffee and then think other. Determination to avoid the definition takes nuts and beans and roasts. defiance is Saturday to an empty gut and the witness of expert nearby to slot. It will be more interesting to frame the question, get it exactly not. Actual answer will come from godly bouncer, the truth obscured from the most of rot. Lighting indoors, crumbs are beneath, anger mostly valued by having something to say. Celebration of complaint, exception. This point relevant to central joint. On the wheel of done, this means a solution. Had it been told, remedy constitution, teller fuller of compromise to realise. Table clears between courses, double to dropping rocks. Man really knows what he does, doesn't have to think how to. Acceleration is glad to see an early leaver. Co defending mule gets up with her pashmina, leaves. Another co defender is a man with a scratched nose, all those present are valued for exemption. Gallery of capability makes way for lolling back succinctly. Arrival of service is second as none other. Raspberries mean Two Ronnies and they could mean fizzy worries. Quantity of three baklavas is better than yeses from the waiters and the experts and the situation exerts. Man in contact and so is the woman and the aluminum and the curly hair. Congregation are participating towards the corner. Maroon carol is opposite to straight ahead. Who could she be. Coffee is hot to the time of being drunk, certainty is luke warm to cold. Acknowledged nightmare is worthy of porridge, being square. Clinical imagination resolves the situation, put that there. Could the fold fit to outburst, oversized outcast. Slouch is custard pie, accompany. This verse has value to purse, could become tiresome. Living in stare observance would appreciate the distance, newt able. choice not to spill is optional, enthrall. Good side to baclava is to steam on and get complete value to finishing despite cough prompts on continuing. Baclava has treacle and green pistachios, raspberries for greens to contrast

Versacios. Waste of leaving misses the guest meal could be won if talk was at a test. Ambiguity of no chance is decided with volume' lance. there's nothing left in Somalia, there's been a dreadful famine of persuasion. Moral tribulation affects the whole room, its' not just the lone mule. Pig in the corner must be of the domestic variety, sympathetic to company charity. Hurried exit of push chair world must not be afraid and risked on pearled. Great explorers carry the flag rave of human charters, well known are all at risk, even by product. mule would sell transport, mule would herald it, Crusoe and holiday to proximity. burgundy carol could be Ezekiel, could have relevance to Carole's treacle. room is modestly balanced, wood veneer to rainforest. finish is tarnished by having s to stop, top relent. What was the limit. Slash back and separate link forty five investment, the code and reference numbers are insouciant. memories of booths here to be more sincere, folding napkins more weighty faster laundry. advance of space makes Brisk at ease, Russian could be Italian. Lady like Dixon is only later in Dixons, wasn't instantly. Puzzle is sorted with fault, snowflakes individually vaulted. Match sport is outrage, winner to a team shirt. Casting crew similarly new, they don't see. Empty suburbs twist the giant key. Helix perspectives to flat; none of that. architect try to ignorance buy. None of contestants will follow the gnat, or will they. With first apparition, Gabriel's right. seeing a flood go wrong with a doubt. There should be no angels on the high street, future trends. right of right is wrong with friends, only angels. Most significant viewer doesn't have cables. most upside down boss is paraded, that says box. Face next door is not as heroically guarded. Applied perception doesn't mind officially. Liberal opponents begin with sanctuary. There could be bathrooms for romans. Shall not say no to the question for no. Shall not say no to finish the yes. not affirmative or negative substitutes. no and yes as lovely. Answer detection is everything socially. Lean back marks of insincerity. tip numbers to dexterities; there.

Some things don't go through when they are there, administrative touch. Release from jail. yesterday didn't write. First thing to do, rose water on Regent Street. Clue about wetting the restaurant. Cornish pasty going to prove to the land of Covent Garden. It was not going to help then, it couldn't . Second chance should, could. Would would happen if the drift wasn't set. traffic of where to cross should cross to fix the save from loss. Oh well, oh well could be the style of tell. whole paragraph from lunch has gone; wasn't important. women leave and one says absolute chaos. remark is the best side of how to think; what's next. happened to all the goods at lunch, covent garden west side punch. Happened to the choice of save, somewhere lives with constant rave. Eyelash curlers mean something. Paris Hilton amuses Frances, she is stupid, clever and tacky passes the point. Not being hungry eating anyway. Old ladies who stay behind are not entwined by leaving sharply. Big finger in the ear, big nose on the finger, shoulder on the hand bag, ruck sack rearranged. Scarves across the street, people and how they meet. one with purple hair, more people everywhere. Seven year old in scent, are you alright says the chain down the road. have a sniff, have a smell. sorting out past oh well. done is done reminded from shell. Quarter to five is too late for tea. Have a scratch to settle a flea. When do the tramps move in. Saturday extra spoil slime; could be confiscated. Prizes are starving snails. If only teas maids knew what they said, they would bolster flanks of musicals. People with northern voices take the sides of fools, gooseberry ones and truffles. Sweeter size of social kerfuffles is allowed, near the gates of doom, near the gates of bride. sodding lunch paragraph took a slide, it was quite effective. Cross under passing, do how a future would. Expensive indulgence above appetite, angry slight, eating to consolidate. mistake sense of acknowledgement, what's going to happen, something pay the rent. At the door, small people hope to take their way. eat in the street and walk with sticks. Two legged and four legged farmers farm, cripple has to watch for clutches that make sense of one. configure interest knows that wearing a hat has to be learned. Borrow that borrow. How careful can the promise be to promise knot that it did see. Swearing not to eat the pastie eats the pastie, swearing not to learn is travesty. Swearing not to cream is creamy, swearing not to that is a hill turn. Breathtaking view is pretty, scarves like jollity. Woman is the mountain thinks. monastery is the fountain. Retain the head of ding parts, keyboard switched off. Keyboard switch off in the shop, why did the keyboard get ripped off, get scoffed, doubt the loft. most significant thing about going nowhere is trusting. in for the cornucopia. Shop doesn't allow access or distress, shop changes and becomes less of a fortress. Shop was shopped for ten minutes of flattery, sit down to any invitation and scatter. Most ridiculous thing about the turn is to answer what to how. If the question is parliamentary, detection is inventory. Should there be doubt when getting through has done its pout. Preciousness with chess. Consistency of time relate to solvent mine. How was the presentation and world mind about invention. Joke about the spy. Funny or the joke about making money. Most are and the place of bad language comes to pass when it swears by word, signed and thankfully dumb. doesn't realise harm, mediocrity swipes a bum. Cream tea doesn't mind fun. Pleasant negotiation. All the time in prison thought about strand and cognition. Stupid spark played game of park, stupid stupid park walked the loop, stupid spark took the bridge with the friendly mac, he's a man's attention. stack the most ridiculous persuasion goes with thought evasion, most ridiculous protective person deletes trash and tells coercion. Man presses red for garage band, it doesn't colour, it shuns command. man asks for press inversion, wily, clever and lonely. Apple factory would not seem to be so with technology, white is the furthest laboratory and the incitement is exploratory. Man says can he delete the garage band, the man says can he play Lan. Sparkle suggests wild suggestion, super agency expression. Small girl alliteration, call spy to entertain her. Poo and the central game of dropping information are corner stone to congregation. Nothing belongs to the individual, however the dress goes is residual. Friendly lady always friendly and expert. Less friendly aren't shop assistants but shop existents. Customer service queue rented with nearly new, best hope for exaction is bridal refraction. strange man push the trash deletion. introspection of fine teas Tim Spark. keen to establish life's existence to his digital cabbage. Tim makes his own application, teaches something like coals to Newcastle. friendliest man full of lies, friendliest service is fond of spies. The Big Bus Company takes the lonely on sightseeing tours. Bumping into things for names and drawers. point about insistency. tis to rehearse with exactly. Good people positively actively. Street meters get off scot free, Home Folder and Hard Drive are fighting. 20th February 2 am. That was the nineteenth. 20th Feb is up against Reiss, went shopping there and touched a coat hanger. Won't win an orange for King Kong, just won't . Isn't bothered, died the rescue. That says did. appreciates misleads to hog the story, should have mended her phone on Saturday. Stalls like the tug of war, pulls as hard on delay. Would know what to say if she had perspective, burning. Sneers art the missy inflection, has asked for a termination by vague situation. Many stars passed away this year, central autonomy doesn't sneer, raises the show to public irrelevance. Drug of unusual things and unusual people is about being normal. This week more in trouble than last when so many things have passed. Crap advance dragon chance. When awards are fixed as legal swords, Dumbo flies. Sneak into the Puzzle why not and write an article about brady. the day is Wednesday, it is almost eleven, let's title. 22nd Feb. get dressed solution about neighbourhood watch would have informal constitution. Allowance to be story signed with greatness partly emergency. In the case of no milk, next door has some. In the case of dog hunger, take the walk out. In the case of looking out for, trouble subsides. Corner work of being true is not pointing, not notting. When the singular question is the main suggestion, wonder is exaction. Bridgedale man, fire engine, quarter to ten, crossing the road, juke box is strapped in the lorry with a safety belt, R593 VLF. sentence begins with t and h and e, a paramedic weirs an ambulance man wearing brown, colour of an upside down puzzle. Alarm polices hearing from indoors, surveillance of being knows no laws. DJ disappointingly embarrassing. Sole of shoe blow plastic bags and planks, dropping paper get no thanks. Computer system stealing invention. don't mind about keyboard feelings. Keyboard something with squares and letters. Pressing doesn't take to speak or mind hoovering. Swilling noise should bother a customer if the opening time is earlier vernacular. most silly place to design a costume for a person that isn't worthy. Most exciting way to live on bread is to go instead. Most mediocre acceptance thank a man for coughing. Most criminal exaction clued up to wondering. Most obsolete man in the industry extremely happy about the fleet. Most red and green and blue, most parlez vous. Story board juke box, word is Nexus. Espresso comes in don't have in any small mugs, sorry. Coins the slot, coins go somewhere for a cherry knot. Infill is the only thing that counts for reconnaissance, delivery waits to be allotted, that word allotted. Bridgedale and courage, R68OBL, meaning about cellars is read to smell. Puzzle is the name of a mysterious person at the top, don't finish the cup. Strength of what is done today may write someone a play. Writer sign the puzzle off, doer does the rest of scoff. Problem with early release is the snap shot. Lilt of fat men spinning the top. Hounds of Baskervilles probably grey. Man o the telly is breasted in a single layer of clothing. Windsurfers rip the waves, curling there expects. Cribber was too good to do, waste is keeping store on do. Camera the most important thing to see. Film on the task. Mohammed is late enough to shake hands, concession crosses road to discuss the problem. puzzle and agent and flat are expediently linked by location, genius about the teenage fan club. Who wants to live by daylight bulbs, who wants to. Sultry headline make adjustments, Philippine gets sized up, friendly maybe, maybe not. very like phonetically. Careless. Arrange to meet loose ends to a representative. represents a dirty circle. Need to sort, witness daily superstition. Wonders about Spearmints, rhinoceros lens. Requirement to touch base with key objects grown up; tag, there. Could be important people in the lift next to very unimportant people. Could be formulas for getting away with things, could be solutions. Bingo hand shake! Wednesday on a twenty second catch, marriage to train with six eight. stubborn cheerio does't mind about twelve thirty, Wensleydale burp, corner stopping on the junction, barking Scottie goes berserk. Significance of good and bad symbolic to trade, agreement with awkward is simpler in fact. curious, clever, intrusive, admirable, relieving, conning and appeasing to invisible things that may not be insignificant.

11

Problem about Lynn. Everyone is Lynn and Oliver, they're all stapling and Gulliver contains a story. Marvel voice referring to the Irish transfer, says the name's as diminutive that would plaster. Filter through idiocy isn't immediately. Lady phone hangs on for details to get repeated on a varied string. How many ways how exact to the phrase, number affirmation, exact or lilted, yes to yup, double five, owe owe, zero . Will be in the red by the time of the go through, knows it takes four days. completely amazing voice to give itself choice. Thinks she would like to. Where's Roy Legend. Anxiety farting is different to non anxiety farting, far graver. 252 and 33 and 52 reside, can be tough to peep for a track. Sequence can knock the carrier back, was that gas important. Willy slack something to do with toe tack, rack and back, rhyming with airwave double letters that that somehow print next door to each other, just like that. air could be something to do with dying or flying or buying or trying or lying or crying. paragraph could be bawled at the security man, knock about find Princetown. Got herself into Fletcher's rhyming slang. Should have heard the key rattle trying to connect with the bank's call. Knows how to live on the side of it all, knows preemption, oddly satisfied with meeting the hone in, preyed on. All the time. Sensation whiffing centre attached to pawns of dispatch, fly grateful to Venus trap. isn't anyone Once in a lifetime. National Theatre 25th Feb. garrison goes by garlic sticks. Any prison is good. One hour of embarrassment. Procedure for admission prefers verbal admonition. There could be a firm story. Tragedy line to parody. possibility like the script said. Swill approve the swallowing curl going to the festival. Pollination between institutions, tourism and the interest loosens. Best practice about creativity getting positive outcome, defeat for heroics. Heroics get defeated first, as they were established. In general terms the view of humanity likes to be ravished. Laws of insanity move on. Oh, Miss lemon the splice is so close to the dark socket, resent bad perfection, stretch puff sparkles. eminent in costume. Lure to heel listens to stay where you are, image is close to steal, rhyme fits the crime. Miss Lemon, thinks in terms of Miss Lemon, the I to herself of beckoning. advice is taken aboard the accent. Miss Lemon ponders to Miss Lemon's inquisitor, Miss Lemon talks to herself like Mister Hercule, uses the tongs of Agatha, all she does is learn. Miss Lemon read Miss lemon, saw Miss Lemon, knows Miss Lemon. Has she ever Miss Lemon. Miss Lemon takes on Miss Lemon, meeting the sight of a bus; there's Miss Lemon. Miss Lemon is recognised and signaled to stop, drop, carry and park. Miss Lemon goes with Miss Lemon's Miss Lemon up to a certain point with her head back, must not spit. finds herself relevant to the air shelter, sleeps under the raid of helter skelter. Does not look at what she writes, independence takes on fancy flights. Grasps the stairwell bannister when she has no notes, will turn into a toaster if she exhales. Miss Lemon is glued to her desk, has the footprints of finger tips. Miss Lemon is Miss Christie, she is an old Lady. Hopefully gravy story cook. Thinks she would be simple if she could fumigate the parting of good to smell its own end. Depends on sensitive friends, types asides for snoopers, must not seize. Miss Lemon feels bitterness to tension, it suspends crucible to serve its mention. has to play Jazz if she is to believe what she has, Miss lemon has the formula. There is a hound, Miss lemon is around. tries to see with hardly noticing me, may appear to have heart burn to give innocence time to leave. Miss Lemon and Miss Marple are straight. Small pink jacket leaves toddler half full. Miss Lemon to Miss Marple can take years. How old thought a puzzle is bought. Getaway clause is holiday time where Miss Lemon went nowhere and found a television. lives with heartburn. Miss Lemon appreciates that every toddler could keep Miss Lemon young. Supposed to board the aging train. Dropped wifery to solve the constabulary. Learned to file, her offspring took on style. Became an empty vase with Money-penny safety mars. Inspired many thinking rooms that earning livings were new shoes. Is better at entertaining real laundry. cleanest starch adorns Miss Lemon; foreign aides to the ides of March. Has rich valves of national interest to halve. Slices the zest of indies, tops the gin precocious. Is younger than spirit for knowing the limit, is undersold to reinstate. Hopes to tell the lip from the gullet, Miss Lemon is a punnet. Is other fruits for all that touch her cheeky sluice. Could filter the mistake of departure, hungry for an archer. Miss Lemon is set adrift and wonders why she was drawn to the sift. Sides very readily with reinforcing captivity. Developed the population. Has just been to see a play with the most best lead as her boss. Has just sat by a table that was long and pretended not to notice what was going on. Sees all the similar trees, is drawn to the hologram. feels teary and thinks about time. Had hoped that saying magnificent things would elevate her tote. Would bet anything to win her story. Doesn't miss what is taken out of her hands, doesn't wash them except with ammonia. Miss Lemon thinks soap is suspicious. Would like to speak French, Hercule is handed to publish. Faces the cookery counter, la cuisine is anxious with feeling. Hand eye coordination reads music. lit la musique, publiquer la music par l'air du temps, porte des gants, Miss Lemon porte des collants. porte l'export du feminine queen. Miss Lemon shrouds dowdy, nurses malady with inspiration warns. teaches windows with styled awnings. Is on her way to the capital, not exactly holiday. Oversees parliament after hours after the tragedy. Preempts the tragedy, wears lemon skin. Tastes liquid pith, grate. is webbed to the holding, prone to ripeness. has the answer for the chooser, beckons selection by grasp, how particular. Lives on the island, exchanged. Rearranged in bowls and rolling pins, far and away the obvious sign. wonders why the readers eat her, happy in her tree. Would drop if she had the chance, she'd not get picked at all. Would like to be touched after all, painting in the hall. Relies on her name to be recalled, can let smell and taste do the same. Sounds like the four other senses, she's put in a puzzle about the sixth. Observes what she does, fingers in gloves. Has ordinary grace; mistaken to place. Would see chip custody as Friday's catch, would enhance with far less fuss. At a distance, Miss lemon is impermeable, sits in the back row at the front, gets a boiled fruit and pulls off stunt. gases at the palms and doesn't move to faith in calls to arms. Has been naughty like an eavesdropping plan. Doesn't fall naturally, and graces the table. Pot and show. Relies on show what she should know. Responds to the pitch of having the taste. on her own has no animation, beneath the station. Gets dropped with the book, the wintry look. Miss Lemon goes out of fashion. skulks with static prices, has no shares. Spoke old time dares, doesn't have a mobile phone. Glued to history's imposition. Wants to eat fudge cake because there is no brandy. Withholds primness for depravity. Miss Lemon is probably an alcoholic, she wouldn't not think of systolic. Finds terms of embarrassment in shames, not familiar with showing values. embodiment of deportment, does not see the point in pretending. under sort has not time for cowardice to flaunt, has no need to act. Acted by encouragement, strange creature like a tidy squirrel. Miss Lemon is squirrel Nutkin, doesn't dine with picnickers. Followed by serious imposition, season. Wonders whether the festival should bring her Guinness over. Wonders if bringing over is suited to her. Would assume to be dressed with Mr. Hercule, missing the sun. Wants to keep her coffee cup, doesn't need clearance. Finds the waiter audacious, has reason to. Chooses for sticky fingers, marinade used. Thinks the lemons would be good cleaners. restaurant deserted at six o'clock, gone homes completed teas. Mentioned with pies and pastry fringes. Goes with cake, goes with biscuits, doesn't go with Guinness. Ungrateful to wait, should have thanked the seat administrator. Arrived late for the show, only just got out of bed. has not washed her hands and isn't welcome in the toilet sands. Miss Lemon pees lemons, she should. Knows word for understood. Does not use dyes, is imitated by bleach. Scenes the surface wipe, is wasted for cleanliness. Has a gullet that concentrates on higher things, conceals acidic stings. Brands as R Whites, tennis wear is broader than Nike. Has a frog in her throat made of garlic. Lower down that frogs go, beneath the sound board. Sees that 1759 is the level of a harp In harpsichord. Will have a job sorting through the stones with strings. Will hope the olives are pitted for the bother that olives bring. Hopes to catch the train, missing for walking lame. carriage of her desires, sits by stoking fires. Thinks boof crying is bowling down the track, Miss Lemon clackety clack. Thirst for a draught. Guinness made from wheat or barley, not sleet. imagines caskets of competition. Unmarried until she is drunk. in disguise classical to punk. Leaves train for catching a story board, has an office and a telephone, has a red telephone. Has cabinets and beige with the onset of dust to her classical world. Although Miss lemon is spotless, she stays where she is. cannot be relied upon to go anywhere, she is the grail's despair, living underwear. is the only important person in documentation. writes down the explanation. Is the seminar, is the fruitful entity without the need of cookery. Is self contained and gets assaulted. Is more exciting than the apple, especially to sailors. Miss Lemon is citrus to Venus. Is devoured by the world at large, is ear drops in a rainproof vest, is properly harmonised. Has to sort out problems that don't relate to her, how to sweeten on the sour. Kind on batter. Swills and hopes to provide concrete charters. is the stone to the olive, catches the pigeon. Miss Lemon is the doe, clean to scrubs. Green flesh about cutlery. Could be eaten with teeth, but the result would be messy. Miss Lemon would Inverness with sounds like . Reduce to eat in her fingers. Could wear a hat. Miss Lemon cuts and pastes the citrus place, swallows on the beetles, cliche beyond her time. Has been classified by a naked man with weights. Has nothing to fear and has been thrown in an onion. Compare onion to lemon like the festival. Jams with doubt that she should grow roots. Hangs by the bough, tentacles know how. Yellow to green, has pigment, proper pigment. Could hide in an embarrassing situation, has the right of way. Knows bulging eyes better than doomsday. Miss Lemon is the actual birthrate celebrate fruit tastistc. Intends to be meteoric, puzzles gardeners. Is true to herself. Everyone else systemic. Could masquerade needing aid, goes blind. lack olive green to find, lemon stones package tones. Miss Lemon is also orange and lime. Grumpy Miss Lemon wants to find the door, she's a canapé but not on a guest list. Stroked to share, conclusion burps. Festival and national arguments go on for every. the product of both is best. Product of best is both fancy. The problem with kinky attractiveness is unregistered. What number maximum office in the taxi. National festival would have the whole pot in with the crocodile, the whole lemon with the saturated smile. Whole range flame digress. This populace isn't the best sense. Century of indifference un rubbished with love. Dim Sum.

12

The Berner's hotel would have coughed at the sack but the scream stepped into a dignified place. Street dribble isn't should. Incontinence count for validity. Only point having control clock the meter. Only way to lose is to leak, only way to Morocco is by boat. Long way round mediterranean to moat. Everyone crosses the road away from the scream, saves crossing the road. choice to step up steps down to the fold. Problem with trying to keep up is saying that nothing happened. If it did happen it needs to suspend. Main trellises of gardens re buttoned. Point that didn't mind what best face thought. Best face is the baddie at the wedding, most handsome and most prone to ways of men and women. Best face is heroic and dashing with silvery strands and dervish like the man in the chicken shed except that he is Kurdish. The only inscrutable fault to Best Face is that he doesn't like to be misplaced. Most people are arrangeable, but things come to best Face for his inspection, BSB to sky and soul detection.

13

There is Susan in the play. She is a genius to stand by her day. Pretty after a few scenes, funny in the first, endearing and full of beans. Obviously prone to potential, like the need to be spotted. Best Face rarely cast, authors besotted. Best face author to circumstance, often a truth of bishops. Not about romance. liquid shadow to what bird thinks about with Faust and his horses' heads. Best face need not necessarily be handsome, he is absolutely right. Best face isn't the same as manly grace, gives women souls of doubt. Most women bail out when they can't fathom their freak, but best Face is quite a man for knowing the peak. When manly grace falls in love with Susan, Best Face was the celluloid cohesion. Best face would have married Susan but realised she was pulling a fast one. Whole cast saw Susan and she had a low down lump of garlic. Awkward excess is nothing to be redressed, one word. Best face is a choral scholar well into the warmth of being right; close to celebration. Susan is in her bridesmaids's dress and wants to get married. corsage on her bottom. scowls from the audience section, deflate lives of projection. Thinks the set up is there to expose. Reason to play game have another go strain. gets embarrassed according to large plantation men, thinks she Would like to be embarrassed according to a specific problem. Trouble with Susan is that she has too many things going on. has a gigantic horizon that is completely enormous to every submission. Should pass the molestation test with dumplings and a vest. Looks at the mirror behind her and thinks the people are similar to people she knew, keeps typing. Susan was Miss Lemon not long ago, difference administrate. Susan was sure to warm up somewhere between Miss Lemon. cool and sheen. Miss Lemon is Susan's mahogany, sets the virtue of chrome in the lobby. Miss Lemon is completely accurate about substance Susan. Could recognise Miss Lemon with a man on her arm. On her own, a world is a barn. Could be vegetarian if she didn't go so well with prawns. Miss Lemon and Susan are hungry enough to meet colin Firth. Would write for Colin and play for Colin. Would give Colin what he read, would jump in bed. Miss Lemon would read the look, give Susan a book. Would suggest to Susan to eat dumplings. this would stop susan's pumpikins. Would wait until she was fifty three until she dandled her grandmother spree. Would be married to her thesaurus and would guide multiple brontosaurus, let the brontosaurus claim Yorkshire without a ripper. would work for golf ball faction and should know the name of the hill. Men with flat, Men with moor, all three in law. Miss Lemon would paralyse her soul for creed, there are many in need. Computer betrayed this definition by Susan's pride. Susan needs Miss Lemon as a place to hide. Miss Lemon commits her distance side. Difference between Susan and Miss LEmon is the same, oddly enough Susan is more virtuous. Whatever Miss Lemon wrote about, Susan can do it either way, its in the script. Susan is defined by curtain time, plot by dime. expires when the amount for cappuccino prefers filter. MIss LEmon finds Susan disgusting with her wet socks in the restaurant, Miss Lemon is never content. script to succeed over what she surveys. Is what Miss Lemon surveys, there are human problems. Is bound to come up against the practical need to have imperfection. escapes her room by Susan's intervention. Beer tastes too good though the spirit is too soft. The only relevance about turning is left to eat meat. Main opportunity for animals is to graze the vegetarians. Replete at a certain point in the food chain. Mushrooms would be good again if Susan drinks what she does. Is subject to plot without having to pass. Is the institution of law in solution, lives in Lincoln's Inn on the Strand. Goes to watch Susan after work, likes theatre perks. does not do this by the booth, surrounded by Hercule's proof. Miss Lemon interchange the weathervane. Hercule undone by youth, is employed. May not be employed by bad pursuit, Susan awaits it. Catches what Miss Lemon discards, passes on the men from Mars. Miss Lemon can see mirror for what face holds, Susan shows what Lemon sees. disregards nine o'clock with elimination, case hopeless. persevere reason. Thinks surroundings are definitive, has no ulterior motive. Must explore as far as she is able, is largely blissfully unaware. Best Face the interface. Green curry for green Susan, started with mushrooms. Green curry severs either in contention. Difference between Susan and Miss Lemon is the general public. The General public goes to a dumpling, eats red and green after consumption. Could include starter, twelve minutes past for after. Miss Lemon and Susan inspire starters and mains. General public think about spas. Susan and Miss Lemon go to sap before everyone else, and even if time coincidences, choice example set. the main obstacle is circumstantial. General public win ties to Miss Lemon and Susan. Miss Lemon is paste to the apple key and V. Miss Lemon enjoys privacy to the attempts that she is won to be. the main generation hope Miss Lemon is employed for their benefit. eavesdrop violence is safe with Christie, posted on a sleeping message board, isn't safely desirable. Fresh meats walk the planet in gucci shirts and secrets. What are cakes for Lemons and Susans. Public houses depend on games and messages.

safety of supermarkets choose constance with consistency. price about treats is not to obtain, bargain of wealth similar lane. Think how Onassis must have lived. Best reliance take imitation from appliance, spin of machine is reliably mean. Man in audience did something disgusting, ate something white from his ear or something. Man in the audience did what nobody knows. Man in the audience went out to buy a dvd about the picture with skinny Sherry. Man in the audience took out a loan, bought more drink than he had blown. greater reality to recovery, all morose departure from skull duggery. man clause that it won't happen. Man in the audience may have gone through a stage view. May have his hopes swamped. Man in the audience not sick, only due. Man audience saturated a meter, call him . Assume someone near, row a to zed. Prices dear, company emblems. Happy behave or rhododendrons. Resort theatre stays at home not to risk the egg beater. Constantly harangued by virility, paternity, spend the mend. Would like to share. Hollywood shriek pass custom bleak. hopes will prevail themselves from retentions. here is fairly unusual, distance prospect. What do people do on the television. Education raise expectation, auditorium suggest middle action. Would only do pantomimes in Glasgow. grown from a Grovel. regular often absent, send Half with children advertisement. Eighties would not afford the time, nineties summon prime. Suspect world project, average daughter no worries to slaughter. Dictate fancies are fakes, mostly right. not necessarily tight, retires to enjoy. Work possible to enjoy berserk. Leave solve smirk, clean to attend. No use much loose, may have to face up to uncomfortable truths. Thinks menus are safer, too much blether on racer. wouldn't want to wake old pretenders, advise for boring Miss Lemons. Boring Miss Lemons are entertainment, they haven't flowered, haven't engagement. Engagement makes Miss Half Lemons' into whole gooseberries, quashed smoothie solution. Half Lemons take time aside predicament, aside to lonely advertisement.

Half lemons aren't consumed like whole Lemons into Susans. Half Lemons are more like Miss Lemon than Susan, country safer detriment. Style of dress important as Miss Lemon because she is vermillion. Does not reckon outrageous. Spreads fashion to be contagious. Revolutionary party in Spain during the nineteen seventies is about Susan's wane, left stage job and took up plain. sadness passion deserts sensible reason and Miss Lemon is freezing. Miss Lemon awaits to send her children when friendship readership. Dropped in Barcelona cares to read. grits hone in on scores, Lemon and Hercule in drawers. grit grid and Susan sandwiched. Definite word ratchet. waitress Hot drink grown up, morning look up. Hot drinks coffee beans, consumed in the morning and in the evening. Hot drinks continental, blob on top trace. warm room great heading. monkey stairs have monkeys on them. Pass peanut pairs. Wonder about play boy. Act waggle their ears. Go into things through hide and seek attention. Release from prevention. naive from wily coin oddly. Shed away current blast. take on the agony aunt, become plants. May be good at saving goal. command didn't mind. Frightening feather boar defend and build upon. Haunted teenager unaware. Bow wore own. tassel the hat progress. Live in a flat. Disappoint support, not much time forever escorted. Redeem by winging up the bridesmaids through performance. Bridesmaids can be pheasants. Disguise may not realise. Quite proud of grandmother when battery runs flat. Miss Form unlikely recipient of beautiful norm, pass by with her friend, saw it all coming. Cause moose skid mark. Way into the dark, failed the test and must seek beverage. Leave building with hildebrand. shamefully modest to the punter. Shame as a nazi benchmark. close glowering toast. Quip brilliance exaction, not part of the action. Beg extent give chance. Edge of seat occasional glance. sees man with a disgusting habit in public and thinks possible trait. hears instruction Stay where you are. Beside impressed by the beautiful sound. Thank you very much four seats left.

Good wear vest, budge in the interval. Doesn't listen pointedly to all help. Is an eavesdropper. Notes musician and the bits the hand sweeps. conspires that she has hires, doesn't know where the buttons live. Tries to walk into the eating out house on the first floor. Man from behind her knows her. Walked out at the sight and said he was full up from lower down. Didn't mind and carried on down the stairs, obsessed with stairs, never used to be. Took up worrying stairs in her flat. Did worrying in the job, but was left. doesn't mind stairs, often climbs to exercise flares. Thinks odd name, not one she would have. plays when push comes to shove. Saw Miss Form and carried on behind the beverage trolley. Could be cousin. got told she'd have to pass the Form test. Miss Form left school less than half a century ago in terms of life. Miss Form is a problem for, so is Bertie. Bertie comes in grown up and drawn. magnanimous enough to include porn. Proper problem for what she scampers after, look there he is. no better boyfriend, closely sounding reading. Promoted and holds the umbrella. More than look at me. Liberty to how some drugsshould be. some hugs does drugs and beetle bugs, gangly thinking. catches like the Best Face big bother cruising. Makes out she is bullied by having to collect her own litter. Pees in what she thinks of. repair foils, leers at the tsunami, cosseting. Doesn't admit and then does. order good for art. concedes fit, masks superior knit. better than Miss Form, Best Face. Respect for staking out job that used to boast. Better with so many layers of tragedy. Potion goes home and has a not bath, sees a miniature quill. Dark feather of Sade's park. sat next to quiet absorber, handsome enough to understand a private quarter. obsessed with privacy fulfills ventures abroad. had her laptop snatched, with realised knowledges. Awards sympathetic cleverness with looks over her shoulder and glances in the mirror. Knows the world is equipped to do with forgiver. Thinks the worst thing to reach is well in the clear. Sees bull dogs and scorches their prettiness. Admires accomplishment with ear marks for IQ test. Inclined to get sympathy from tough gristle. factory make angry the home variety. Mercenary spatula brat on the cover. not that appalled by the festival cafe, looks at the flame, chooses seating to watch. Thinks open kitchens are designs, thinks benches with padding are umpalumpas. Wants to be nodded at by waiting staff. Gets laid by comments to like. sees Charing Cross. Face a hike. Sympathetic grumpy frenetic. Very vulnerable turns the corner, and then she's Constable. Genetic enhance when book shoots. Gets excited revolution ignited. Breeds capacity for love. Dismisses her own love and doesn't remember tough shrugs. Comes round heart of time. could have worn special shoes. If genes are cognitive. Thinks bag pipe man plays for hot coals. Take out on oats. mild disgusting dressed up. heroic clover. Stock up mouthful work, deserve quirk. Deliberately refuse to stop being revolting, revolting. afford fatter over weight. In a hurry going nowhere to marry. Curry is out to get her, so what if its nine o'clock. Tepid stock. Half laughs at friends, let down with distant rage. Proceed trial long and arduous, stretch out marvelous. Could be friends with fairies and cakes but subscribes to relying on aches. Only jolly cross. Wonder soars what she does ignores. Notices womble ways, audience anxious. Fantasy womble actually Grumble. Suppressed earthquakes in the form of nightly wakes, wander in dreams and mystery deeds. Probably being good even though the story is. did should. Chances and doesn't chances. Excited by chances, doesn't. self discovery easier with motherly, needs man to point plan, find escort fix fake tan. Goes arm on arm okay better than single gong. Finds men using, gets left after tantrum. gradually only. comes round on the way to. Hears the Stew. Wicked hears words for. resolves to write them down. This helps when it goes to town. Thinks fudge swapping vices with nudge. Street crooked, walk down and mend. Walk closely behind saunter behind tinted windows, spend plan on forgiveness. Point to make by walking down Regent Street. Point of good in three dimensions.

Walking Chad. Doesn't own the relevance of poor little rich girl. End of that sentence. Basil craft of syllable. Measure that shaft. work out what poor little rich girl sounds. Pass on next rounds. solve when sell, listen in on passenger. Doesn't want to feel unless she is giving benefit to her wonky keel. dignify sleep walk ties with wanting to find out. Outsource message unpleasant, isn't escorted. Swears to herself, invitation riddle good to block. top shelf about pictures, fancy miniatures. concerned about screen, prefer soup to steam. Doesn't know what happens to her, diary wants to hear. Secretive for good reason. Sunday no time for apples, holiday thought. Sunday is mangos, fasting to sup when hunger isn't more than dinner. Monday switch lions, channel mastermind, jog a bit. program antique's road show. dying to go. Dribble woman feel strong. Breeding challenge blame of expertise, copyright. Resign to channel hop, snack on chutney and downfall stock. Something to do with compote, cereal and being on the Billion. Hot bath at midnight quarter and quarter past. Tension uses where's it from. Worry about property and people all wrapped up and down. Checkout absolute. complete rage somewhere. territorial about settlement. Knowing movers are bound on Da Vinci traps and cocaine. Hoist twisters and hair gel guess.

takes a drop in on conversation to

'Say saw she didn't'

Thinks she is related to intelligence. Bullies are translators, friends, people she turned down when she was gutter wasted. death and responsibility met. Politeness more important. Hard done society tries to join the Que. Tickle sobriety, check out glue. Make boundary anticipate. Fool guru and huddle. write guru in full, write hurdle in full, not be angry about the problem. check forget use. Saint as an albatross. Pin wing chivalry to the age of piles. Usefulness of seeing dirt. Clean guilt about personal. Unfathomable nickers and boobs. Response to these tubes. Deserves to live in a bottle. So there. Nationally proportioned family bound to betray, word invented by people of dismay. Ring tones with famous cause, grill is a place. After all the intention. Appall place tumbleweed apparent. Sight of wizards with dismissive coughs and scarves very welcome. Sight of establishment raised from ton. Endless address pass through, living maitre dee. Place quite empty, full as well. Tidal wave approach sends forward smells. last four word fit. Different left behind. Filling restaurants rhyme. Debutante Point about targeting features. dante spiral. Did nobody mention Orpheus to Orpheus, says Orpheus. Did table never mention table to table. water above board when it runs. Water run over. water stuff between countries. Land backward flow of what went by. new settlement similar to creak of door, things that happen to climax suspended with Timex. Presume draught postpone joy. hearth spoken for. Presume exact stat. further behaviour extend reach of learning a bargain. Carry on past finish, wind emit greedy establishment. Influence behaviour. On occasion time stop caucasian. Easy for categorical dispute, apart. Saddling what comes, hope in shed. May want to stay in bed, go abroad, place for treading in street sword. Persevere against, train SAS. Target can be set for poorer Margaret. Boycotts apparent. World could be simple about blot from look out. Every time there's a horn, others drop a plate or storm. Drop a plate in a restaurant and get rung up by a phone. side step respond crepe, fill time in step. Constant monotony isn't the word, constant obscurity isn't the word, constant goes with correction, correction minds correction. Cohesion to sentence has temperance, lime pie cheesecake. Banana republic of Katy moves up a seat in bad news, closing down junk food stores. measure of business in shares of children. Healthcare bound to save water in the toilet, surgical need to be indiscriminate action. Wrong sort of progress tail off headline bad practice, world isn't Pharaoh's only tax avoiding Nero's. good work cheap and cheerful. Summary policy since when. Most tidy about communism, most complete about giving in the sack saying never.

14

Eidelberg is here, borrowing shelter on corned beef humour. Move over fatso tablets with chip savoury and Mexican whip chase. arcade attends to counter. Song begin in b, lathering margarine to bite frequent snacks. Fallen crust slabs throughout journey surrender notes of tea. Talk spread on ham 'n brie in France, jam at home, anchovy for other people's fridges and sunflower spreads summer. Trip various liquid on Tony Sheraton searching for panther. Go on at last, in written scrutiny if the session opens. page on Wiltshire time survey opiate birthday with current study. Breeze persists outside with Spanish literature, good man was once in Hong Kong, double sides turn to page two. Wendy struggles upon a character score of cream onions pre washed and ready to chop. home dinners that people watch on TV benches as she watches them dream through. It is not certainly bad weather that gives winter a name. Convection begins with C, substituting N with autumn's Brighton. Blackpool's brush to Bristol creams in blue bottle batches born to chemistry. Pen lifts nib with curious hand. back to ashes ember the grate logs. High Barnet's wandering soul fuses tin canopy from thatch eaves. persil spills for gravy. Handicap shelters eyes from browning. Stalling crows fleet overhead views against sky. Birds fill every page, flap, flap. Feet score trample Peak District. Rubber wedge curse the final answer worn in labour. Bethany does sums awkwardly ten stones, three, four, five caught a fish. Alive, seven eight, ten and back again. Post stop marches lunch hunch minutes even contours. Halliday trees malting brown leaves, twenty two buses to Wandsworth. Three old friends ago, ramblers invade positions without queue. So says Bethany's vest. caption organise constrain with car puncture. shapes of gutter and wearing. Bethany is not responsible. Police respond flights to blue arrows of Sherwood. this fetches tights from harm. Ovid met Ulysses in Latin after Greek. Maths before lunch and games asserted on first breach of term. Welcome Finchley to Ogilvy state conference. Inlay proceeds with stylo glen pocket. electrified since the last war supplied peaches for a dairy. Vegetable round up. creeds bullion standard at Friday markets from Thursday. Enlist flavour of Stork to save Uganda. bellow yellow priested wireless. Ask busby instead of Busby puts Busby out of a job. Rain sets in matches, bus load meet for petrol but weather fine intercession. Young prize volunteer laundry needs collective wicker smile hosiers for Tracey. Pier in export. Tell joke now, lend a hand. Bosworth says little Sevcik. Polaroid moment in fashion. Interest fall on Nasdaq assembly to subscription, breeze carries on foliage. Mildroid picks her nails. Flower on ceremony in courtyard. Tilda copies Louise's walk at the factory, motioned by Kurt's boots. hobnail floor standing brazen. Muscovy ache livid jaw for Brian's load in sympathy. Scan page in upward loathing, inconsiderate Victorian age. boot foot Michael Hazard. Copious deed. strings ledge hedges, encouraging civic bravery. Sparrow slit parody not enough. Barnacles are enough barnacles, even to sea resorts. in July New age angles the support of separation. Kevin shape won't match, embalm evolves. Show times open days. Give Alice practice. ability to blend hardship. empathy to Dickens, Wordsworth and salt. Read sea groins as a snatch of peanut butter. delude a tame gull into friendship where boats don't sail for seamanship. Please break the riddle, cry shore master tiding urgency with excited youths. date against safety. Uncle calls lip service with the freshest breath there is. Gas boils up a hearty roast toast with Twix n boast. Gravy searches for missiles and avoids peas and carrots. Contrary Sunday lunch coverage of the Bosnian crisis. Where were we. Continuum Castigate Project. Almond bank statement perform disclosure.

debit in forms of leisure. Gate Where Cynthia wanders amongst transactions. purse buried later. Only freshness permits invention. Madam Hybrid expects persecution to explore. Log feeler construe the board for a flat landing. graffiti ennoble claim. place must be exposed, anything from John in a dining car foreign to him. not know lines, pouts contradiction. Raiding must be furnished. vestibule worried in the hall way. seated throwing kitchen parties. transpose after beds with fresh seasoned ventures. next day in history, no wonder! Teach fencing to guard, telepathy is unreasonable. fleeting looks abhor crow. There goes necessity box of escape, martial stranded on communicative. Jump Lez bee frenz. Several packs meet upon heather because some weeks are permission on fallow plans. Please move to Australia rolls three dice. after vegetable rice and biscuits, nobody asks. Mr Speaker does syllabus well in court. Pass the chocolate pudding. Layers gone over to increase the definitive outline. Sprig of holly on quack. Impy, skimpy parlez vous, Gideon buys walk to Odeon Radox. Still being there in five years time the path wends along the rock face river. dike on popular hedges and long grass nettles. Still being towards ham for lunch, house adjourns at four before five. Advocate Ham, spam and egg. Tow pathology visits country house, done before. zion even earlier but best gardens close early. May birds weed spectacles untended to wilderness. June's stretch to September. I bought a pair of flip flops two years ago. Ladies and gentlemen, tip this way. France is a stalker, bonnet, beret, Chamonix, vanilla cream ice cream sundae. pasta pesto never heard of suet, gruel at mascarpone, grapes and cheese. forget mascarpone, never mind dishes other people spread. should be gruyere but comes as mozzarella in stretch limos of nourish supplement. conversation no good without it. Peanuts, spam, peanuts, ham, dish of Spain in gammon. left ventricle, clothing right apricots on tooth picks and honey coating. Somebody took the wrong leg and the world caved in. Fifty two weeks, a few spare windows and endearment stagger on. Everyone hates you, vexes Sophie with a pen she wouldn't buy. Paper mate 2000 stick med, nails need a trim.

15

Life begins in a dormitory to dedication. Obligation to finish a pen infuriates the environmentalist. Ants are on my side, but I won't crawl. Humanity strangest militancy. hurrah seems pen is a traitor then. Pen swears oaths upon bic back. Plastic stick thin nib, broadway rangers, odd staves, buskers. Iliterate please write home with skill. Brodie hobocrat, given the paper of Aspen. Donation follows with led. Investigate source, don't serve creed. Biro clearly discarded to make a pointed apology. Impossible some pears gambling. dog dolls uk. Eradicates move me on time to quarters on their way and mine. Both in a room together. well done in wallpaper's window. Transgressive verbs of doing well. Elbow Boils. Peter shy about the taboo that Dr. Doolittle admires. Periodically woven into Peter's arms, pop through anxious fault, none other. Insecticide begins with I and ends with E. Herbaceous borders propagate the eye and nose in summer. Care taken when crossing the road. difficult Vanilla ice cream. peas in a pod. Don't shut the book shop! paralyse and fix the adventure! Don't laugh at my sworn headed outfit, don't trouble, don't contradict, precede, exceed, resemble, enquire or placate me. TRIO bunny dough rob in son.

FREDDIE SING FREDDIE TO ME LOUDLY SLESVIG AND HOLSTEIN AT SHORTBREAD DRIVE CALLIGRAPHY.

16

One hundred lend you fate for notey joint. Late arrival custom late so so is on time. Welcome to the slab, watch faster than expected. How many shepherds do you know, sheep, shearers, shenanigans, shiites, chevals, chaperones. How do you do dawn treader. It thunders outside, washing on. Drop on the floor. would five twenties do or one more. Permission thrown on poor so they have to use slang. All worst sins are cloaked in cunt, cough. DJ name like Stace that may reach porn. Borrow loo get analog. hot tank, cold tank, burner, septic tank, cistern, ink, bath, candelabra. there was a time. Three old ladies stuck in the lavatory, Monday to Saturday knew. Work in chip shop Demi fries. Work in factory, plurals please. Custom emergency stands for permanent ink, more aside for yourself be you injured or escaping. Maketh scientological claim in knitwear. Minority failure, Tar macadam toll. mad at sea, armada on land, both in books, both in class. then laid an eggy one. Hullabaloo capsize. CEO album, Artemesius always philanthropy. Hop scotch, trestle move, clear bombast, extra trigonometry metronome, pleasure Louisiana, insincere. Doodle explain passage goes. not read in lines of sound. Maybe the wire goes in directions, that's all. Reluctance with recollection leaves A,E,I,O,U at one twenty one. Section obligates pride in chemistry. Mislead current statement to claim notice and appeasement. under the sink is liquid gold, and Peter tires of cousinhood. rock stars fabler mission of radio times in symphony. Be good to yourself assorted crisps are onioney. apparent claim. This works for Julia who affirms a proficient keyboard. Relay Mention Eisenhower and snoop cop a string. Eat cake in quarters. Consider bogeys as professional slime films. Radiate ether to sons in law. pastry at least once. telephones an earring sale to

Van Gogh. Remake examination, strive against curly parsley and maintain catatonia. fixing the aerial. Strive like hard to take. Of Use to Birds and worms. pop in and copydex feuds. Caterpillar. Roamin' inside frame. set drip formula . search calls and the tray slop sensor. case brawl filing pews. second number seven slips over. Sit the overs, ban clovers, barn hysteria with acknowledgment. Tape overs with hysteria, land the clover, stand in parsley. Fix the wedge, mend the sledge, furnish deck and mill the hedge. Jessica reach open practice. Pigeons coup the loss toe tags eating bread somewhere public. Man in house cover mouse and gin. Paint coat indoor.ssolace against will. Dinner on time. Interest in tragic labour. Sore non doer. canopy with foliage not clouded water. Green case absorption. Glow worms glow better in darkness. Level crusted wax. tend to Arthur Daley. Gran marries a Chippendale. Tea at the joinery. Carnival slang bingo, keep talking in hearing incidentally. Cocktail. English native corn. fetish to sugared water. Bowls and messenger crumbs away. Gobble door plasters by sweeping tins. wax polish guessing weights off linear countenance. Pretty upkeep, Santander. Arabic, Norway, galoshes, treacle, pest, flavour, temp. Box shows a colour of oatmeal. Who thought you a study ceiling. pokes on mythology. Hearing aid mangers crop the ripe fingering. adams rib on molly coddles prayer. species gives private hunger to empathy group established with Aberdeen Angus. cow prairie. System one hide cow for solder moo's recall. spell onions and gravy for next June. moo gets branded back, scorch yells moo. kit for jacket. System creams bond for weather, same goes for cotton. Instance one is much the same but for Geronimo the ice is cooler. Discursive of signal failure, but field drives through moos being heard and tawny faced. Cuthbert's fight lasted briefly. mend rattle on the blind. Cuthbert cherish adventure but give cursory fusion. Simple agree with torpedo force. Tooth and paste, gleaning from cavity. Nowhere that fly yearned for him. Other than practice by weak forces. Deck chair indicates

Doberman. City with innovate balm fold. cool sheds. Side soliloquy junctions Garth with keen attention to special effects. Abscond red bicycle. Minion order participate eventually. get drunk and comb. Seating plant to organ. grinder Stavros. Guilt shore past legs in rows. edges on a gangway over there. SORTIE on stairs. Is this how you speak. Job interview according to plan on the fifth and sixth of spring month. Ten a day attend panels of twos and threes. Sensation gives reason cascades about circumstance. Second round workshops prime the counterfeit. Speech only to those on team spanner ships, crucially turning sages. Begin open bowing spear. Custard add later please exert force. Miriam's daily men scrub potatoes, thinks for Bollinger on leaving trains. passenger floats. boiled oat simmering on fag sharing. fag in Parisian twills, duty free blonds of loyalty suck personal dry. Bryan Adams multiply top song. West life in Roy's membership of the book club. nominal to profession. Grizzle chop imply enthusiasm for youthful grace. charm's length reach over and whisper a joke. Caspian is now in charge. rooms go freelance until cleaning. Operate plain friendship, apply soap and disinfection. Friends enable hands as flagship stores. mercy keen unruly. judge bummer hammer adjournment. Goats cheese. Isabel must eat cheese. Leaving school's folly is wide open. devotion to paying scoop and role. Earth wind and fire, bar ain't Africa. Loo Chando Bid. Your book was brought to my attention earlier this year. gorgeous Scooby sends it packing. These notices find trouble, roof exports, silicone trips, marching pants, jezebels, Matlock, Sidcup, Everley brothers, Jim and Sue. Spots of wax on my floor bury the chip. scrub the floor back to syllabus. pass Go for standard returns. its the best way forward. Can anybody draw. Blowfeld mixture assume a green farm patronise stag bull. chain from flighted sparrows. Gather round at later than noon to spread cheese with chicken soup. no chickens kept in cubes. land rovers shack the concept, smart land rovers, keeping ends out of minders. Cajoling the rut lends gravel on bad weather.

Say hello to Alice, hello Alice. Alice, are you queer. Do you have goes. Alice looks back personally licking a green one and laughs. Loans to parody don't fuse with sitcom. Distinguish knee high to failure. streams and lost caboodle springs open. How anyone could know. Tell Ordinary forward capsules. inconsistent with marching. Saber tooth dog, neo, kitchen roll swarms and a trip to Crieff after. Professional's pang with brush strokes, things happen somewhere, itching pledge mundane. the right cable. scorn every pit. Question does it probably, moments of shining, I'd say. Ramble kicks on to the home strait. everybody does it with a cleaner. Down across Friar is straight shaped. yoghurt, hello pot plastic. don't talk back. milk in a bucket, breeze tube. Duck drake, skimming ponds, leaves in the moon ever grew there. Grecian urn, pottery display. Hostage and peace knows Aquarius. Keep doing the shapes, Mr Kinesis, avert all sentences. Something caught up with me called the order. That's how they explain flu lag once brethren pass it on. Sylvie comes knocking. downhill note reaches the floor. the only contact. Marchers from Butte pledge Lilly greenery hands. Real syllabus is for cantankerous names in pinafore. paint leaves with a hill pussy of skin and broken hieroglyph. eight thirty bar tenders on shift. best pieces navigate what. Kosher cruel with ended backing tape. Don Juan again grinding coffee. digestives wheat bacon flour bacofoil. Tomatoes bananas cereal pizza bread sausages yoghurt spring rolls bananas baps Jif ketchup peas T roll pringle scone nut tuna chicken marmalade sweetcorn baby bel dog biscuits cauliflower onion henna brasso coleslaw nurofen fairy crisps rose sprout earl grey olivio tea camomile. Difference kept in car boot and out of dusty blue bells. Once upon a morning star I wonder how you are. Throw away the Stanley Kubrick! Scrape off wax. Comb hair forwards, tie laces loosely. never mind Nathaniel's persistence. Marathon stranger imagine the picture we are looking at. ALMOND WOOD in SPOON 40MPH What the issue at speed SLOW Go 5 laps EXIT.

Sugar and coffee joined up writing. Stubborn experience get
a bargain, 99p. Give the name to Marcia, hatchet cry birds
flee. This is what class sounds like. Nevertheless anyhow short
changes a superstition omnibus. Help the aged seems a good
idea till Feng Shue voodoo kicks the bucket. Specific Anthea
doesn't join a community group, instead prefers introductions.
reliable source attains grand relations with adventure, has she
time to kill. Youth doesn't shit failure. Stainless.
CBBC PO Box 8999 W12 6WR
Slightly poronographic. Need of description. Farms apostolic
eyes of closer supply. need wants a market. may be fresh
vegetables to talk of. Glue bind manual value. walls and
men decipher late. appoint to catch a paragraph. In so far
as shoppers marsh, confusion swell abhorrent wiggle and
trip lethargy among bounty salon. Thursday gone spy mark
of queue, tall and black vexation, moderately timed on one
to miss. bringing here's menial compare chance. jostle that
despair's marginal shop. will re-fit the order. Stand fraction
adjourn and watchful keep. assurance sink deliberates. Notices
and whorls of term. Fitted smock label times again. Stack toga
eternities, common colds, spraying seeds. get the biscuit tin.
Lurid chase on winter skies. Blaze white sovereigns of parlour,
gammon shake's uncle was a greedy pig. Confederate earls
munch with jam. Settle for sprigs. Enquire what with muse
that food. adorn most of the holidays. Wheres are husked
beyond notice. Pays sentence with extradition. Later ones
enroll smithereens. Grow lean and segregate more acceptable
toward, if not by the decade. Descript soul by ounce. Lever
baby foot from babble on ground scene. Shadow multiples of
crack and stain. Share company endeavours to mine fever.
conditions restore. Name composition steely. fright the
lackadaisical iron's old bridge. Millicent's blunder upstream,
ever the scourge of minerals plain. Cruciform oath to span
a moon. sucks and ebb commuter gloom. Always north and
south in a hurry's remedy. Colossal sanction dandelion. marks

eddie the good wage of inference. Like some buyer's guided hand that discards and enslaves. Has to feed the labour. Simeon's disguise patters among chenille misconceptions of card. pile. Odd squats board squared papers. Inky stead that tapers. Try an endemic purge on a maestro. something or a car door ordained. By thatch, credit and recently suave. Inter continental stones. monster ocean floors in plumes of enrichment. poisonous gas recently snare's option. Demeans guided. Trace that revolves daisies and wagons as objects of marvel, let theirs alone. Try filter over that, present authoritative jugular vowels. redress beverage for autumn snack's equality. Scudding reprimanded for describing swallow in the vicinity of paper. maybe latte no sugar. Lady cue's box weighs observation to entry's submission. Rule no drinking. Go level in coffee, lack of apology and infrastructure. Paper cup won't lend. Name to paper, ward of example quandary an illicit act of rebuke. Reams of slur ascend. goose flight, marvel flap opinions. planes where men think. Generous peoples quote induction, serving mood where synagogue. touch cares of nasal mist. Babyhood, writing mongers a severance pay's injunction. grow landing woes on cast. Rod ahead that may be pried open. commend hook a snatch flume. Thicket from bee, treasured and shaded. Elegance throws a glassy stare, staved form rungs of adornment. Minuscule clapper beg diffidence in cruel effusion of sandy shore. Carnival B to B's A that A parted from Z's finale, scrounging new turns. patch to italic in Garamond, lean from churlish times. Deuce compliment advancement then corpulent action foraged with hay provisos. Semi latte daily. Yet, lusty lords, I have escaped your hands, your threats, your arums and your hot pursuits, and though divorced from King Edward's eyes, yet liveth Pierce of Gavescon unsurpris'd. Breathing in hope, mal grando all your beards that must rebel this against your king. To see his royal sovereign once again. open country, Gaveston pursued. Eventual graduation leaves Meredith time

to take stock. Curmudgeon slicks of haste are tender, enlisting
a sandwich course of carry a folder. links of hole tenure
seethe revision. doctorates coursing with life on sensibility.
Young Frederick was drunk after the play in which danger.
Thousands of tiles threaten bathrooms of exposure. Olympic
stealth crawls sheath to fry batter scones and jam in readiness
for bath time. Its funny to think about screaming, melodic
to outward bound and the screech of laughter. Commiserate
wheeze brink the choker up to air frames. Light junction seem
among mortar stores for distance. Presumption here calls foul
whereabouts. beyond mild children, amending souls from
dreaming. lumpish gwandwanas. Choreography is a count
at hand. Burgeon heads for bloom disclosure based at camp
and excavation. Fulcrum's Norris hasn't been heard before,
as if light years are impending warmer climes. Route 419 goes
every seven minutes, news teeter crumple inmates of milk.
Curdle curled at fourteen winks of march. tin scatters furled
by slobbish gin, yikes. prevaricate guild a stride for inertia
and substantiate. serving stencil trackage handsome loaf.
Ponder the square abode's mundane calm. Requiring flare
pieces of chintz. Ring wontons and prescribe anchovy. Curb
marigold into lending. square not the route. Homeward with
inexorate knobs of meeting Wendy. Crevice cramp cosy, fun
throw liquid, spots of garnish. Quarry adamant give chisel and
pasted face proof that sores hills to rubble. Not friends. maybe
squirm through hatch. radio arpeggio, carving tunes enjoying
the same songs. Banner forceps rejoin surgical frame's lullaby
tristesse loop, choral symposiums. Esquire in flatulence. Ovid
gets stuck on plastic scrolls. finger spread jam. instead lay
formica, learning renewal. hopping magnet and porous talk.
Emphasis of height, spartan chairs, disappearing walks by
linear ears. the whole party of conference cheers. Exception
nook response like button rows in flowered heads. doing up
cardigans, tapering collar and scruff. Bellow crisps on stilton
hum at five point scrawl section, corded fuse. Peters,

Fraser and Dunlop Group 503 -504 the Chambers Chelsea. Lots Road, SW10 OXF.
speak prang sequence, bump offers of criterion. Library in place, scene of hurt, spats of paint, belly leer, bunch of posies. Gradual stair top pages, bob to castelate dusted in spree pickings. Bind staves of strand, sheath engage. term dry deviant, arabesque. Everybody reads the yellow pages, van fronted, mostly English. Root position, first inversion, second inversion, base note root, bass note, bass note. Facet gripes furnish blinds lipped and flushed squat. Occasion seek walking vestibule. stoned along a bank. Greeting a range by soft furlong. handful scruffs of plastic peppered sweats incline. stern dew position condemns roast and malady. Oregano's colour earns flares by right then posh crisps in culminate route. fail gullet thus done alone. Redress in action. Threads o' series back in locum. breading out pads of secure vision. staple cross paths and Catholics among rhododendrons. Most blossom becomes fly's jet black. Laying Hertfordshire with Faberge, survive winter. Time allots the suitcase in mannerisms embedded in providing the best handles. Strapped in transit. Some o' the scenes see farce episode as a joke of their belonging. lengthily explained among parts of national security. bound with limited attrition. Welcome back hybrid run for decent bog standard. As with funny string pi, millionaires. Regency teem debate, half wit straddle both reply. even distribution dissolving soap. Step code bereave verruca, puddle and cheesecake. Marshal stamped in ignominy at the reach mast practice. sooner torn than spoken. several sheaves switch. Top copy tops dispensation among staves used for boarding. Black spot assemble glide fractured slate. Lemon rind. instructive manual from side to side's casual mend. Sort of iced beverage from new refrigerator. Cobalt screen undulate harpoon of ghosted stare that guess parlance on history. Shakes, compromise like margin red. Invoke caps of steel garnish. plastered on ignorant. Stage wasn't it queer to go. By

land avoid fort Knox's end of hue. Question stride along plank of ignominy. Portrait shelf of Dante fame repute with repute. Spinal track and ladder of dicey snakes. So lend a mouthy rung. Care of board. Turkish nasal smell. latin and cognitives. LAMISIL at 1%spray.
Bread every morning among villagers of swipe. Dress labour. Used to be convection geographically. Epicenter toast raise cheerful mountain, brew life corn. Apparently not intentionally. Choose book skinny begin again. Arm askance with folding red. yellow page leveret bound by extremely interesting need to present. Other colour from glare elude current stem. truly original. As if anything helped foot steps. Plain to Ned is the lease. thank a silent ebbed cord in view. Proven appear well spoken. Tax fledges. Insinuation tract claim, sum numbered. Figure transport lively. It's from last year, pending April's tray. top deck's a scrawl. Every decliner saves a ton of salad. Cooped upon cans and corned beef. Fetish washers of curly braziers. loop eloquence on haze and garish. Shake horrid hurt and square the till. Mini embankment. Squat mute in languish. literal to love. Ingratiate progress enquire accumulate throws at blank space. cavernous once of spoken fools. Leg of tether, fully minded in lunge. craning view. hopping, cycling against the mill. loath to write in curled down cork or coal in wormy spiral. Dime read crooked tow in hand for latin numeral. Instant neighbour churn postal incandescence. Gut concert un amused with non commentary. bead bread and jam song fowl. art jeopardy kernel pew. B and major minor. All three quit staccato. approach reason with spots from jockey leather. ungoverned enclosure. Trawl find all anticipate. Sense of way look anon descript. tenure procedure is bounty. Ever men stow to rupture. Multiple story in penguin clone, worried about the waves, hailing cabs and dogs. Worth weathering lightly. Level at swerves, heights of bucketing. Drag slide squalling prop. subterfuge. Hurried shelter set busk livery. vantage central but crawling. Chime of

burden infidelity. Watch fob and split coach contents. Wonder striven in contemplation about the station. Transaction precinct. notch grab in confidence. Scaling polling headway, triple vaulting. Questionnaire in bold refusal. unsurprising awe snatching open gob. lines of spider glue. Jovial buoyancy lay eight quid and candy. Opium, Balthasar, stolen freak lag sky. Lean in for wispy hoard. Thousand hand of three impacted rods. Casted feather grille. marsupial stones, and laughing cheeses. Custom endears cedar grow nonchalant. deciphered of impartiality such as Mildred's scouring wash. Space on how to please commend exfoliate. a little rude is younger. Stark slate for obviate. Simeon shoe gurney lace. sprinkle un conjoined. Trench, menial peel, foreign bogey, learn the word piazza. Obedience narrowly adjourns. chance to spice. Melody assure word reveres. inkling only case. Mean yes in a certain view. Instead, all puckered, less pretty. Shy scores less remedy. Is a panel that copes. Bubble goblet proceed the condition. Mauled glass in hot pursuit. cracker biscuits, larded suits. Yarn will spell failure presented by patio crisps. that ye are emboldened is not usual. Twelve three tabs of code to mend. Sheath elected and ordained in boredom. Listen for boredom. stowaway abundance is. Ha'penny won't offend tuppence. Fiver, leave a share bald. Ever the sugar pad. clean on a sticky walk. Brine Pattern. elderly ripple at Bournemouth. Cord lean while introspective. jitter Fish sandwich. Netted heather bone. Gathered up. bar still guard water and city. Empty menial question. crops a choosey float. Garrison bar with leather bench. Cellulite from damage. Segregate peer to lever actual tongs. Apply treasure norse legend. Twin log prevaricate. Brown radiator and gurgle. Suppose after mints itself. Story begin with providence. Material of ink spurning bland sanctuary. measure with spring. Pomp hasn't made its mind up. Well no matter where it cleaves or what for. Piles of gloom crave archangels to bed. Tea like the day's method of closing down. Dashing men link polar palms. galloping women exchange orders. Bath tubs rubbing spots and choosing work from scans array. Placements etch the summer city. Pursue languor on a hazy lawn from fearful of denominator. No hero but troves. Preclude journey's end magnificently with televisions for peaceful meals. Its not so bad that swallowing is an art form, castelated frontier. Warrior gear Marcel eats toast. weather's bad, mentioned like heavy drifts, and the toast goes down. Forefathers pit and polish with ergonomic finger. one in the other drifting. Fork lift stare a cold and northern Narration. Moody flare splay Reams in The cupboard. gum proffer hunger sliced no ham. Malteser knew furnace robbed, settling patience. Brick at stern procedure. elemental order, Marcel's thumb by city of long poles. Inventory all in masked attire. Modesty Large struggle. Furnish layers abide. Open sky, opiate in brevity. Constant and none gauge. Hero isn't here so school gets on with it. coat fit and stable numbered for seating. Lap lazy way of window. Plot creep among players. each song harrow and sip. Someone in row four. Plot portray number two. one two oblivious jacket. brightly cuff, say marry the two. Vision what's between. may no longer and get set. Strong Jezebel bing bong thunder clunking. wordy name prayer the wanton call. gramophone bibbed in practice from those of Sharon. word wreath at the hop. reach indoctrination thanking swimming. way from a large boat. Everybody affected by next loud front. rhyming weather target. cloud creeper for holiday needs a subsidy. obvious broadcast cleaned. Projection with private sketch. editing seen prescriptively on a lonely trellis. massive pressure familiar, filching to protection. Swarm track teased with censor, tingling knees. embark enormous, engendered nonchalance bring in the nonchalance, the spark has yet to yellow. puff pastry wend the scavenger. Sword in half deserving. breakfast Marcel's finger. draw hollow in man who serves Line

'I am here'.

best man for job phones through. Intercept time for

friendship, better scripted than transaction. avid play already
married but willing to resubmit. rascal run good intention.
The city has been worn. surveillance cue and guard the fraction
of the eat from civil unrest. mall fold Uriah's clothes. tab
junctions of competence. don't fold, Uriah will arrange. Hobby
replica go for publication. singing tarantula human. Mercury
prod at the mood. general for A foot with five toes. waste
conspire. Breeding a walk. Slice leaf a crush among
themselves. Indoor read a metaphor. splurge among the breaks
of chapter. bring coffee to a stand. Plume in honourable dread.
Dog against tree. Articulate stride among and among.
archdeacon promise to unfold civic guidance. verbal carriage
in warm August supplies. Livery strap headless elves. brave
with patience gently, their statutes mostly contrived. farm in
squares, hybrid functions of meddlers. Garden apricots at
potatoes with library membership. miss the despots. arid
consultation nursed on beds of gander. safety empathise.
Heraldic work mend curious. leaves all tame. Somewhere
better, finding the digit. Consecutive offspring ensconce. fare
of all for embarkation. reluctance describe opacity. spot moon
on by another sun's light. Spare ferocity about, jobbing the
legend. This happens now and again. concrete now. shut side
meet panel. Curl swindler introspection to the value of one.
Margin overdraw seating the curry. churn an equivocal night
in piquant fix. Spoon hunger thereon; now and again. herd
words, coping barns of rice and barley. equivocal Harvard
cupboards swapping receipts with lip. Chastity Hoarded
blandly. clusters of nougat depart, ever leaving barbule strands.
quavers hunching. Contemplation unmentioned. now that tea
serves pouring water. hotly lit, positively sparkling. meal
portraiture place attendance. require the side of beef. subsidy
scalpel, grey smattering. conversions imply wet and British.
was the measure. Seated postures to go. Lunch in Remedial
excellence. cools with fortune. Temperance does not stall.
tenure's pace with sprout and bean. reward potted ivies of

concern, lightly strung to puddings un boiled choice with fresh berry counteracts. Tuscany napkins helped. grubby with seminal works. collectives peer through some fable. fist of knowledge arrive, hardly driven half doored, and the bull gored knocks. Monday's flower answers despite the dear wall. automatically witting lazy blinks. remonstrating unseasoned root survival. Story Un mechanical. pledges turn starch ridges. Presume shrunken gains. unlearned, inflected and fluent with syndrome. rate exerts the end of term. cars drive through, permissively. scented ties pan language. luggage port of minted oak. envelope millicent feet. thereabouts a carnival. pitch and sentinel. lime and soda reading aloud. grasps Having sped a throng. perjury heard the same already. decree at mould advance pentameter. flurry bold sold against tenses. reminisces on cuban missiles entreating chase to nurture. abominating under brim exposure. Maple care posses. shuttered in sleep and glorious tone. point when pearl stalks a living. composure on sharp election. parlance's stream eyed commotion. Whatever lighting centrifuge. coded morse inspires a condition. after the initially good idea. Suing the future, marking wrens, hooping county bollards and lunging exonerate guilds. brethren mottle n daub on small Carmichael. Smallpox keep felted Lizzy on stairs. sooted in history baps upon Consonant. open doom a shaven lens. It has often been the way to take stand on third legs and chairs. Make no mistake. I have a voice on a button. Sets towards game the shares. Bingo's fetid over but that's every Thursday. Regular caller, unlike Jehovahs. make their welcome in as much as bearing up. sustain for years at times of civilian alarm. Heaven knows theirs are squared. My custom to condiment goes with ready ketchup too. garnish covert operations. best left indoors if you know what that the dog eats. too few bones that are legal to chew. Some call potatoes and semolina the bollox. less current than steady bread. more urgent than chicken nuggets in goals. Toasting in winter hibiscus, deli oat stakes. humble dink in Humperdinck and herb, dead man's arm of yore tweed and sick note. When Baxter arrives, say pork pie, do chicken n chive for Celia. when Mable's teeth fall out it is rude to stare. Persecution goes with flare, its not enough for sirens to end there. I say still into garden ornaments and curdle on Sensodyne. Drink straight from the bottle is Jean's appeasement. Ring up Wendy for a vindaloo and some bourbon and tell me what she chooses. Its that spam again tell her, or she can forget it. Very menu winds brew up a tenner, including start ups. pleasure behold square meals of miles in malleable chamber. Boris breathing all over a tether of dominant stream. It fixes resembling. read the quote over Betty and score a Christmas turkey. she said lift a goose which is why I thank her lucky stars for sailing. skivvies all over Vivienne Westwood condiments giving scrape from all fat and fancies with a regular glowing elbow. set up approach, all gurney and swatted to another Monday. know patience apprentice wear and tear. Micro biotic came through in Paul who sold windows for a while. served nickels of cub soaps nicely saddled with constant peeling. Botox stained without sunlight, but only to plastic appliances. leach mineral in a different stand that Paul hasn't time for. So those were my earrings all covered in custard. Limping on, they fetch gastric shoppers from their tawny pink delusion. some of its indelible. Ingots merely smelt ore to the time of pleasing. glancing becomes an art form, decked and loomed for a quarter marshal art stake. Biggins does custom finely. Tulips to pearl succulence. awkward leers off a harvest. So often noses grow out of joint but what is Carthage. Abominable to be polite in society. Nathan scurries to a party home. There is nowhere out in peace and to his advantage. commune admits two to his favour. gait for all that make elder-flower and fervent loves. patch embezzles a certain fondness for beef all over. Britain and decent clocks from selving. Norwich Union is another, goes with Dolmio but the name won't show on the system so render the soluble patient with care and attention. Chelsea thought about the earrings again, about the demolition of mime, and her currency for a decent kitchen fitting. There was no-one to ring, save that of bright water and interplay that was coming to hand. foliage has never bothered the aliens with all that stainless steel and what have you, spot checks. Millenniums come to pass with no greater crate than new settlements. Golf is up to pop tube crisps, time to ring in the score. Teddy remembers when the whole feel of get well soon was enough to build a nation. ignoble compromises well to the service of being cheerful in a modern stack face. Take fatty's dog for excretion and the walk becomes not so low. Fatty's brother tho' he may like the Gorbal's junctions. show of survivors. The secret is a good one on top of disease. Ectopic is a sharp detail. Marion's face is a cornucopia, and education shows it but the film isn't good. engines of tennis fuel a station. Backwards and forwards for all boys called Rory by the lion that precedes them. balls in waiting in hay. Customary toss of serve, does well to remember bake of shoe. black tar and bruising. Just as Darius always swore there'd be jam from his mother, biscuits are eaten all day and tennis does not rely on marmalade. Esplanade Garth traveled a lot from politics to become a foreign passage. Halting often follow a maiden flight and then buckets cry from a factory that has blown them down with desperation. Garth was high and low on earning and seed. Men don't come of age now but through crime. Plays of war and government bounty can't fix a decrepit store. so real. canopy flare has to come from home growers. Solid arenas of debate educate the youngsters. wiser Hypothetically moulding, the great incarcerate of school and work drives the teenage widgeon. Few provide inclusion into the sordid world of cheese gout. until the age of cure it rids their better stealth. Focus on bombing the rose bed, Clarke get mowing Jim. Every morning from the cockle shell is the whir of the sea. March beams, cement gives Ernie his rosette of practice and sheds go down with gin. Another national concern grips the station, shelter slavers on conjecture and Bethany calls in negative. failure try. Shorn again granddads hewn from D day disgruntle balshy stacks of post brogues. number alleviate spurn the island sure. Hogmanay is not best practice, vital that everybody parts on terms. Ring up legend of millennial construct, small consort goes with a party animal. Cynthia names readers so Clive it is and fusion welters. Margaret Drabble becomes readable at sixty, just as pasta boils in salted water.Those are the nails, that's the cabinet, anti clock and lock them out. rotten planks, gloves put sauce on afterwards, lettuce roulette, pig baths in sugar soap. Cooker of loose screws, plate with a chip, angels were her saucepans. planks as if she'll ever lead the blind, turn right then left, bending the tool kit, screws and screws, scrooge, appetite, chopped onions, scrabble, how the rubbish ties, pots, fish eyes, flooring, funny umbrella, gave it a little dish pony, haberdashery, Ronseal, the hammer is yours, my tongs, the stock jug, keep throwing, that says oak, ladder danger, right handles and left ones, fixing, mending, altering, planning, dog on a mug, this one's safe, those are yours, bathroom tiles, a good book rarely, hand wash, substance now there's no fairy, destiny pauses, always use fairy, tin cakes why those shoes, rubber mephistofolese, George's boyfriend, June my neighbour, things recover, work top, fly pajamas, orange ones, jeans, my nails, grit, scalpels, pictures. circumstance go with dreams. pan came and went. Sofia popped Jeronimo's bench, tools of the trade, I give you Quintabelle, lady of the lake, dusty jacketed ones, there will be hamburgers after lunch, Tracy goes forward, Nolan sisters, half past two. there's a baddie working, Spanner random, the real story is brunch, weekend Spain, glossy magazines, perforated staples, Cunningham brands of shoe. Eliza and Bertram fetch pansies, name of station, unfolding, three musketeers, car boot sales, tagging on, helpless gesture, receiving think you, watch telly, thank night rider, read a forecast, blow the gale away, next invitation, private gloves, drawing stares on the landing, Jackanory, pink gypsofola, baby names, disguise regards, crystabelle, dynasty french windows, on call, bystander emergency, relegate that will be nicely. Introduction another word for beginning to middle at the end. New entrants flabbergasted by treacle tarts, cumulative wealth gathers aboard floor. escape for their concern, eyes ensure marble stairs. ultimate no gay consort can agree to differ on arrivals. standing in is negligible. Tardis lock labrador with an inch for strip glass. Minefield tattoo ambivalence to a margin. Savvy attempt deconstruct collusion of self investitures estranged by nominal fees, and that one a bastardly nature. Legs shouldn't pattern predation on hunger alone, they argue for the first lime. Aspect look promising for Steiner. Nobody could eat a thing in sour meals. All's well for hungry health, un sliced not fussy. Civic prides intrude pretender for a keepsake. I'm not the martian from nether region for nothing. all agree apart from anarchy who begs politely. margin. waste goes out with heavy duty, its alarming. Lemons inside bowls, FBI winks. Sense of smell chance the gathering of one desire. It came from Pandora's box by a channel number nobody could mention. Hot cups of tea, all round mirrors began to wobble on crutches, delicate lace and fine gin were laid in the ante chore for what was sure to proceed as a daily sepulcher. Lance of unharmed joke rocket equivalent pairs to reason, posture and corduroy mead at separate ends of the room. Earl fantasy fetch potato groom prawn cocktails, cheese and onion. Green fly dapple opal fruit, mince beef turkey and farming method harvested concept. were it not for a straight approach of Chuzzlewich. Groom recede into trays coerced in humility and a big parade went consular. Hack of sound advice lit podium. tinkle Dale Feeley supported with humanity by shadowed elocution jowls. Songs for all time surprise the rush of live wire associates to ambience, and the girls were all pretty in reception to relevant heirs of choosing. Marvelous catch bristle with pulp fusion, summon extrapolate to board rooms and chartered ocean liners. Best friend Libby parked carefully to avoid an emergence of style such bistro. correspond upward phrase, visit only passing and engaged as a good stalemate. right until the speeches. Phobia claim but neither did secrets to neutral red shoes and matching coats. This was deceptive. Fahrenheit welcome. caution analyse frugal attractive to cakes of occasional empathy and particularly crucial to the emergence of such investitures. Comical inlays of creamed spinach bring Lebanese ways to fodder. not food insist tiring limbs onwards bohemia babylon. Crush silver jettisons upon memos to retirement, jubilee exchange so current with new median safety. Cycle expectant ear gorge seclusion to nexus. real attire friendly fable mask, velcro comment. no carrion is wicked to an understanding. Pisa stands as a firm classic, masonry falling danger to falling masonry. Spaniel trot about in favour of warm hearth. bushel wild for scampering on. Circulation also has poor posture. Marcel dread pile with vigour having no complaints to paradise other than lost without a christmas agony for spending. world in flux commutes route well. poor boy read about staples learn to unpick clippers. Worry sessions on hegemony justify fold's election in spray. Strife unmatchable sum, wanton for talented crash hats. One voice, one worn, one turn. Heat burns on video tape placaters as small jostlers wend refurbishment from a misconception that people intend their loves from banishment. We found the wreck amidst it all, having taken leave on a scooter, in a different market, that's all. Revved isobars above board and lodging, heard in bouncing cricket and throughout garden. Nebular explosion lampoon dairy farm. Clingy sort. If what Mr. Wilson said. True to form a beautiful tractor. Improve job on an old year. Appliance of hamster of spin. Gent yarn donkey at scape's brunch and soporific. Blue coated sprayer Petunia's poor relation. Old sack whinny on all fours. Wheat of modular heaving the wife and spencer over trade. Laws of boredom

which no doubt explete. phrase wail in time, keen to express. Scones more coupled than split. borrowed afford beyond the turf. Affection therefore custody. Vernacular in gland lived upon telly downcast, set swoop canopy to shade breeze cad. Penelope elope even without cottage fencing or mending order forms. Cows jump at night so the season always coveys. Glean in drops. laugh party moan copious compliment. action redress baroque, tendency suck and slip according to height. Poor Mildrew appreciate lesson with only too fine a heel. measure dog with wedge and Poodle leave no talent. there go three and a dizzy head for numbers. Gloucestershire parties were always cruel to their guides in the manner of boot men to foxes. Cunning bachelorhood from stakes of Griselda. Be nice for a helping. Learn shank of squabble against ribaldry. Mistook late succeeders. Reflection and then the wasps gathered especially at the weekend and bank holiday. Alarm Cleopatra into growing wings of fancy. Later than medical action. Squint assume the worst is through them, bringing the eating. Languid shoe grace skittle wrack for better tomorrow rotations. Opportunity spoken aloud. begin implement of cup and wood on handle. Most appropriately, cherokee by Lauderdale plasm but then nobody dies.
Drift goes RSVP Honolulu.

17

Sunningdale for half the year. bought a castle. thoroughly need and when the cue came, seemed a happy visit. Those ones ring those ones over old bones. Steroid measure plate in tow with septic tongs. Mildred arrives careless as usual, modern fathom pants in the boot. Jangle trade with tweed, spank edge on climb. Oh hello usually does it. Nice to see you. Then round the garden for an iced bun. Cuprinol tone ring round again, modular Hugo sit in a rut. Monger sign ons with badges. Completion of My family and other animals pause. Pond fence look at each persuasion adjective. Carlos understood intention. honour by decree waddle off the American trail defense. Several billion gnats on the Hebridean coast, clean finger nails and biodegradable antiseptic wipes. Secure shaving trillions. Jack black pony tail shuffle off deck to reach Academy Narnia. For those upon the eastern pore, boy felt in hat. Penny dare you. Then about wisdom, grass upon convention here. Ryman plastic carrier bag, by your leave. Nepalese antic Look back at collection. bail folk lore in symphony. Declare Little baby rose beds. Add nincompoop. Blast herald recovery. tinge turn stones. untangle for half an hour. Crush carrot and swede, oven in oval. Discourse lend harpoon. Amputation promises me that courtesy is on hand. Sub terrainean gastric flu. sizzles before teeth in fat chances. Quarter store in daily care. precious understatement. Mask mature on crime. Caster sugar equals Relief landscape. Does not equal Christmas every day. Toronto Sherlock bit bonjour. Who is the party Ding a ling for. I want to see them at correspondences. Galapagos. Mental ones show in stanzas. Words owe a wriggler. Escapes on summer pudding. Berry cream roll. Get shot give. Caught as wrinkle dream, worry a furrow. Linguistic stzeraphone harries to a rabid gesticulate. Sorry but even the europeans get a look in. Ban cunt in burlesque banshee. Carpathian squander study obtuse arrears. Silence tongue. Legend Chew on fat, Schtum. Wembley rises, nerve of death threat. split arrow into orbit. Moon for a cumbrian still. Jonathan take notes. Spur persona pull to action. girl alive indicative. Decibel parameters all. capitulate sanguine Beecham. Extreme norm sits to paint. Flora, Marcel, Fiona Marrakesh. Yes no hash potatoes. All play by substance. Mild botanical extra guests. offset large and small. Emoticon when Lavinia crops up. Chip fat spatter about castle Camembert. What a display. Sure enough ski in a yoghurt.

Holiday Katie skim home. One latch barge on grand. Archipelago for Dorset and loam. Goodness, gracious, and great balls of fire agree to differ. Measles, quarantine, cocoa because I am right. sure as hell. Chocolate write nothing about other snacks. redemption at hand. Wolf melted wrangle. impatient Matthew frigates. Palate as grains of lacquer. Ivory grow a Magnolia. shades again. Installation tumble licking it upwards. Impenetrate logs. Cradle view of normal point. Ecclesiastic wenches furrow in Hammersmith, duffle togs of leather hoops. Condition drawing pins in golden domes. privacy notice chase those claws. LP brain honour levity. friend cushion ear worm. Heidi on journey's end. riding hood blow cover on grand decay. Shift blood o' moon. black to quarters. Combine mileage to drag and curl foliage. Safety bask in Wales. Maybe castrate the rate and shovel flowers. Granny caption window seize. Drizzle on counter. She can't see them for men. Sea tinkering at sauce boats with jangly jugs. Fix begin Bisto. Old mother hen crack a tomato. infra red pistol make breakfast. Deer nibble weather bark. Below tree line shift expression. Moor of character. Foreign legion inquisitive. approaching weeks. Charter fares and ticketing incredulity. Vintage parks of storage. begat cask Napoleonic truce. Twist ribbons in bunch volcano. Basil pepper sauce. Lava set chocolate for hot bananas. Aren't any volcanoes in this country. Drinks are generally a good idea. Legless is the caterpillar. Feelers are step sisters. Last year we went to Chamonix full board and chalet for a party of fourteen. Modern vestibules and linky Velux loft conversion. Standard pave the blocks of white scree. pole live for elevation . Expression sealed eyes. arena goggle spectacle. Bahrainis bought theirs with flower essence, quiet boogie navy speed. Coerce energy at clubs. Focus drink in commune. Rare speciality pervade floury top. Whisker unbeknown to try. Keep quenches at length from depilatory creams. Medicine from screeching. Anoraks and towels together. Governess doric pillared, batwing legs in muddled hide and play. Jump under Dorothy, ingest card. Dog ramble on clap zip up a jacket, put coats out. Cheek lick off lip. blink flick sniff atrium. Marilyn goes very fast on slopes of Driscoll. foot rub and corn remedy. Nothing grows in winter, best keep moving. Shostakovich and back again, Columbia proof timber leg. Loretta borrows a hair slide from someone in class. No crockery on landing, one Americano. Knuckle nosey finger on loan. Bono curled hair. perspex carrot and quotient, oat nest bars. salad come a white bowl. People manage gradient with hands on rarely. In my day it was buttons black or red could go. Draughts lifting. No room chair on the sole of a shoe. Forgetful on a Selfridge bag from one down. keys and laces down the far side. Jeans turn a cool room. Legs won't sand pockets. Pole stretch confidence, back stair more in use. Mobile point measure half way there. Forty five haulage more illegal crockery. lip strong ridge collection. Glass sleep removal, few more scarves and hair go by. Pocket thumb china tinkers. Spec max and safe way handle. Brave blondicity. Normal Snap a table top. still punch litter. Rifle index and debenture. bowl originally clear. Plied injury open hoods and strings of evident noise. Miserable at eighteen is flabby. Floris of London perplexing wraps for aunts. Jump for for kicks at the festival. Muffins for eighteen again. Willow spare tour along the top then earlier girl descends unjacketed. Puffa shaded India courted by leather. Back up a cappuccino. Green display irk tropical elder flower. More bags and long leathered husky, modern husky of cow to pony quo of statues. British museum grows a cathedral, rounded scarf with fawn tongues. frond. Clean dried collar sheep and more moves of difference. possible upon the landing of woven etiquette to convince the passage decor to open tops. shuts that drive the gear stick twiggery. GCSE a mark over forty that would blend over. Men all round in peace rooms of sleep and bald parenthood. Two coats under the same fluffy lining. French beret fawns in white suits. track a gym at leisure. rubber band won't stretch but half a glass. Lady without shoes. It is quite driving to negotiate alumni. Two in plain forty fivers. non smoking carriage negotiate bays from e-net trance. Euphoric presence of overdue baggage talking in weight. customer luggage rarely extra here. Hold all knit short escapade across cobbles of glum aluminium squares. Painter strip warden but for this bench the drink is parked on sorcery. soluble wrap nor cellophane. Au pair abscond to crawl after life on box of fruit cartons. Decade upgrade spending for organs. Liver on Guinness happily but pubs are less by leisure murmur modules of company illustration. Environment confuse by liquor, pills are less dribbly. Muffin moves out with friendly pairs of brush up mops, one is in command. Moving factors the observatory ghosts of the lighthouse. fingerless gloves of constant illuminate pads. Sulky trattoria elects a miserable reason to voice imperative measure. F-ing standards blast out from the snow machine, please be-shackled groins of acrid lather. Hot spur spring tundra. Advance from barricade. Lazy Earl Grey dump spend by former occupant. overplay tenancy think similitude to keep cheer. Bucket chair lengthy business but form is well remembered. I keep fresh Rosy and Rebecca with hints of curlew. Fairies fine pond stews of minestrone. Every real to the able. Spare pictures conglomerate. mushrooms and bananas feel chastised. Pensive sit drawing Victoriana, goes roundabout. Pepper tin sprinkle dance. foliate bins un peddle wards. Ping satchel bikini. Feel for a blister. walk continue all petroleum. cradle sapphire which means no rest. further Tepid Casey. roller ball bar tend Moses in flight. snatch coffee toast and jam. Grateful recline one store. ten cups of sugared and salted. Everyone disapproves. at least breakfast is Bagged. arpeggio conduct Lloyd Grossman.

18

Ornothology early bird. Thornbird, quail, turkey, cuckoo, hummingbird, sand snipe, turn, starling, thrush, sky lark, finch, bullfinch, black back gull, wren, crane, pheasant, chaffinch, nightingale, grouse, chicken vulture, diver, robin, cormorant, partridge, dove, swallow, gannet, seagull, curlew, woodcock, goose, blackbird, flamingo, pelican, macaw, toucan, woodpecker, kite, marsh hen, black game cock, peewit, plover, crested swan, pigeon, duck moor hen, puffin, grebe, guillemot, shank, osprey, buzzard, eagle, owl, crow, raven, horn bill, budgie, canary, tit, blue tit, parrot, snipe, ptarmigan, ostrich, harrier, kestrel goshawk, peregrine, falcon, razor bill, stork, phoenix, dodo, albatross, snape, rook eider duck,, penguin, lapwing, wader, house martin, sparrow, chatterbox, warbler, kingfisher, heron, capercaillie, corn craig. It ain't that you ain't seen 'em, had em for dinner or grown to love 'em but worm of a shy poker they don't feed as breakfast every day. Flan shelve a baker's mit in short casing. Message quiche lorraine hasty scrum beaten egg. Council tax biggest rise ever. cold play onion. Garnet, crustacean garnet.

19

Might be rude to use purple in any case. legally bind opinion, but everything is legal till proven otherwise, smudging through glorious trauma's advantage, picky tiny scab. flowers in vase or resign creosote gate. Stipulate guard enclosure, fine metal for back leg scramble. Sag lip edge under foot and gape hand, dog hop through. Walk in park study chestnut as valve to value income. After effect

Perhaps. heard on bales of twine in march. grassy udder grows important. Trundle spouts coastal spire where trees crop tides of wind. Lurk fakery meddle on whether for tea. depend to chase the afternoon. catch on pheasant bushy child. Bundle exact ha-pennies, or good straw on which to sit at the meadow brick. Some houses teem with cattle. Strand sesame and nettle, thistle when boarding Ned. cries 212. plan circuit board, lap Hounslow or Barnsley to hopping ducks. dead begin to filter in the library. first no upset on beaten page. animate with laughter dispute. Photocopy pause at lidded stage. Hand out life's interest. claim. phrase near oratory.

'What I've actually got to say'

doesn't mean a thing but loudness dulls rage to crease expectation. manual gets only so far. hood trunk complete rules. Note exception to bitch response,

'I ain't, Sue sucks'

might be taken to heart. grab escalator by upward tiff about Gary. Brain won't charge and spew. What to wear equal grocery one. Ten to three. One page forward in years. Usually by night the splurge tapers on what the following says. several hundred consultations. Where are you going. Stitching on my right arm has come loose, next stop Selfridges. Van dangling a baby plastic head sits outside our road. Its white and parked Stepping out. There's a girl, maybe a scooter. One time she was a woman that crossed the road. Notice bags in a front minute. Photos friend in red shoes. Board on three turns, vans and bicycles. Tom worried and sensitive. Pass of neighbour flat hair. Tweed cap on a notice for no smoking. Dashboard bluey eyes. Chill morning tread stark night. Smalls in hand with mums and carers. Tiny hats to whirly mornings. Separate flux of day's gait. stop to cross green and safely. Iron railings by lofty trees. Sally doctors or ones that learn. Ten minute roundabouts, each in potential. Rested ankles, just at the flower bed. 'Morning' lift sheen barriers. Tuck the parkers in. Squall of gas purge open care. way to life whatever. Get up to indication. Breakfast by memorised quotes, label piranhas on TV. Sarcophagi fathers in capped boots, clipboard spending pen. Worry trolls a bleak corn, simple con of moving. Don't squalor a hoax reception, graceless nose, narcissism. Walk by the deal to think what squares them. Darted answers. Smiles in self profusion or challenge out of humbug. I saw you on my way to work. Classic group that fates with turkey, meetings, tonics. Whether the way passed yesterday off. Clinch means overalls and bin lorry abundance. Sniff shove supposedly. Upbeat change stride. One a daddy wore up the aisle. Humours of sundown days. Grecian to jerks eat salsa. take big magnum for a show of no feelings. Tasty though. Big man soundly nods intention. cheap cream guild plastic wrapper. Perhaps certify the mongoose, bounding in circles. Treader catch a tale. Counter fiction brave, choose pawn food. seems inarticulate. Ye bit the spatchelor. Up to another lounge. Tinge two tears of glue between walking and counterfeit. Sound without a telly. Solihull as usual, Farnham, Reigate, then elbows and benign.

20

Association cares to mention. Tailor pattern syndicate at lunch. pleasantly seat distress. Fringe in compound. staple at large with stereo pins. Conservatory pat fur, stamp napkin replenish turquoise vats. Consumer shop evenings. confound poetry and art. Workshop extend the milk delivery. section cow mood. parks phobia prompt, checkout the gloomy confessive greeting. refresh switch to lane, market truth. apply choice and seem benign. Buy a complete variable condition. Set of worth and weight. Beautiful day waste to a packet of felt pens, some Polyfilla, roller unfit and sketch book. Online card management enable new system for card balance.

Manageable, quotable, salable and temporary ratings around the locality. Better the seed of a disloyal family. Congratulation opaque among mind. Footstep haggle share, slight of age gargantuan waste. creep their temperate swelter. Medley of perpetual wash and tumble, assisted to hand. Pointer bound to whisper sorry. schedule escape, malleable death if only. Team member, lob centre stage, endless speak on a run, kid in a flood. Separate din. point spend person. Million suburban arrest. pickle jar crammed among mustard pots and subsequent plans. Brilliance hard method, better shoal a tribe. celery. Import to wait after business. Round inscription wrap in glue. Persistence best in freight, each leg to larger top. Stand for planted. between grave and conduct laughs each morning. strain an honest shunt. TV ruthlesss match. Construct terrible clean credit. Should have gone dogging. Boring shouting Arial. Magnificent weekender, gender of course and compliment. Plain stretch a week of jobs. Position tenure lettuce and carrot. Include canned soup. rounds of inhabitants circle the annual plan. Batten on physician. Someone list the salad decree. Little else stretch. backstop haze. Demi day proven wrong to greet holiday. Operation fill castle, none but bricks to trust. Lead stair room. Spate call and knock. bare rise splinter. finger point bolt shut. Larch lacquer and fossil. Horizontal boats set aside on the sideboard. Picnic spots on place mats. Pram ski the leopard. Face doubt and ridicule. Presume same reluctance. pout crane forward, wan cheery. Muzzled, burst hello caper. check whether they aviate. Flout chevrons. compliment turbulent. Wade through blowing fish. Polish preen as carnival close. stare above lids of fresh boxes. Regurgitate marshals again. Sparrow fret with hoops, clamour for a smirk. Mettles of resonance withstand. Upper crust toast garden. Project a most distant event and walk away. Conspire against surrounding, object to doubt. Condemn proper day contract. Get sent back for the usual. Miss a step. Tribal myriad prop a digit. waver equal sum. that's all after a big green monster or such like so tipping scales. Ponder bemuse relic. Bridge original link. squash nose less desperate. Effluent tidy scattered tissue. recommence games. Adjourn to vending. Pleasure jostle. dimple cheek. Trivial by countenance. Copy mend again. Singular flounce, acrobat croon serve ponce. Measure so telephone. Inspire unperturbed and not misled. further from sincere. own. Clout song under feed. Foot expire post. instantly a monument. Consequential beam now trodden. Trail behold deflectors. Martian presume file and preselection. Hurried gate usher unwanted. cripple stop with darkness. house cares. Anger to be forgotten. shade astonishment from hurt. or mildly idle glare. jettison squander. balance broadsheet. steer history apart from nibbles. junket in square packs. splendid favour. continue speckle freckle. Round Arm fancy plait. Hide the corrugation. whim and cool trial. Ikbahl introduce false gain. patience lost in overall strain. Chad potted occupied. each agenda spool. time settle with love. Gorge after reference. arm's length safe secret. hand food about. time to shred convenience. doted inquire of science from superstition. parcels of overture and man came from the jungle. Conservation isn't slash and burn. Deploy survey the expert prose. chase gloom from harmony. expedite new Guinea to New England. age with twenty parents. Multiply in crowds of small rooms. nominate the most poignant and spray odour. Tune Bach and forward wait for commencement. eye shadow in steely nerves. dissipate the most bored aloud with injunction. never permit false entry. Beam and microscope with riddles and spires. many alcoholics breach weather and depart. snails in confluence. enterprise totting consummation. bargain under hammer and tong. capture how ten past ten was an invention. slipstream Galloping incantation. Peaches. I have two ideas that you won't like me which expels you from this examination. revelation arrive out of costume. war torn hardly provocative. Bend unfashionable, value simply written out of context. exeunt. chase on time. tether blind reins for a slow coach. creep after toboggan in leisure. stage grip a mimic. Real players bound like dogs. Doing done earlier. not in the sense of yesterday but less sense last year. not in frequency but by watching old dogs. handsome given the room. measure of streets between. adorn every hope. Pointer extract a various diary. navigate someone's laugh. catch on live in books. ties to documents. surprise a mark with a workshop. common study. breadth among pimples. pigs are Satisfactory. observe with an ice cream. sing to an empty spoon. travel with all the litter. Wrapper broken down. stop for A pen. Hang out the blue to dry. do an airing scrawl. Let the old dear cross the world. Is this a wise move. Let the dish be vegetarian. Is it that they let you. Send regrets that merge. paste the time in lieu. half a pint mend Hoskins you. Entangle striving to be in a good timetable. help burglars. Appease front in texts of bold instruction. Respond and resist separately. mind old umpteenth trend with quavers. Mentally everything's fine. Just been on a trip near Lewisham, not Lewisham but Hither Green as most available train. News of the World put junction in. fantasy in gloom. screen child and man calling together. sickness clamp perpetual passage of turmoil on ordinary Situations. could be more complex than minding trash. Independent repellant on good things, nightly defined to worry actual sheep. mud search. Gated scope seated view. Something obvious to repeat hands. Step through a gilded poem, lily smile. Stem a Giver in the clasp. Drain pages on good sense. slow affair in doubt. reconcile crews as operatives. capture flares in the wind. same stacked in boxes. even baked potatoes make slums. turquoise walks the same route to lunch. whizz tops the concrete rail. computer logs again to welcome but the chairs are new. Same dusky find about the fridge milk and kettle. Strides match tinsel. Fluffy eyes along ledges. apple woman hunches. Pinnochio tends filing to quiet blues. lady was first. Up and down a lift in the hall. Better mirrors and radios. Bleepy passes huddles. ones that pit cardboard displays. Next month Cinderella gets framed and Mickey lies to become her legend. Shutter swear by. Choose silver thread. Lend in bare palm catch. foot stool raze a facial expression. Buttercup and pan. meadow square unforetold. Petal pop to disregard. Stand on end with tiny duration. green by year, sap of cork. leather run above. Jumper strip wool. clip plain bee. Farm crop ridden of old tools. hung about in rustic sheds with diesel and grime. A million summers. Stops of twine the open bale. Horse kick steep hill. Store doleful yell of gulls from sea. Curlew and guillemot. trot along rut and heave belly in raspy leaves. Sheep forward by the road, old women understood multitudes. starry height scribble back. crookt in tow to cryptic fog. Fever wish a shooting star. Chrome phrase shod a stealers boot. fast curmudgeon drives. coloured post Carve in swerves. bend gradient, peel the yellow river. Cat slab for pretty hearth on paper. Shed private waste with shelter. needs all season for above. grand finale, consistent pledge. Registration smile. phase two passes by now that the small sailor boy piped the quadded air. sing to an early rehearsal. gate brand hasn't spoken particular shade of rice. subtle care required on vengeance. mustn't appear in idle thought. Sift dolly, she is fair. walk of guilt and low presumption. goad ferris wheel in sequence. Steady rise steady fall, stop at the ready pier. Quiet discourse, allow negotiate slam. many effervescent spins of bias and irony. Spoil page snag. cue haggard rag. Another something idol. pudding dollop possibly custard. whip cheesecake in company. Passport plate of dill and cheese. jam donuts wrapped in spams of scotch. Seasoned people with delicate goods of don'ts. Mess on by a faulty joke. furnish or sing dues. patter through crust to a pile of marbles. swan token paddle. bank lend grace for a scrap of bread or worm. Buy small peas from Tesco. Chilli are the bird's eye. faction of biscuit cream replenish wares. good spoken for and Simeon is younger. Muscle pie longer and more or less hard wearing.

Disperse essence out of tact. brawl ensue drink in tambourines. elsewhere. upshot remain on shopping. sprawled in tired aisles of comfort. tea in bag making the bus for home. bartering with vacuums. great exodus and back hauling sarcasm. layers glue themselves with baking in a gas oven. Circuit cheese straw. light and flakey. single to nibble, hard to chew. Foliage in plain breath from whirring clouds. gate bolted Once left. stern on Debbie's ears. cross her dog across a park. spoof cure the insight. onion steep in tears. She lifts a careful fork to balance then belches from swollen peas. While wha's mine is yours and give it me so. In actual fact the rhyme is complicated, password for Jessica's separate leave Jessica sultry from a gormless youth. Non gluttanous craving stands to thatch primrose nd harebells. Sleek reeds obscure the brim, there's a patent on what the skirt becomes. Mode then strives off sweat and persil cuts that meet ebbs of Joyce from work, a doric column stair, nag opiates of learn and care. Because the coffee is warm the morning has begun, shortly steep in porus cue. SORBATE, ETHANOL, THICKENER, XANTHAN GUM, STRAWBERRIES

21

Settlement to intrigue. Waste doctrines persevering with notch harms, pegging the goals of infinite wrongs. strange puzzles of being done to. brake Go set for start offs, set darlings of ready to bang. mood hinge harbours. At the little companions. signature tunes of mint interpreters. Saying in shares of declarations. shingling relevance of small incidents. bulging frisson of extortion. Deaf cares none hung. Dismissive times of table associates. shoving of the testament. Mine to this tie. poorly numb with inches of progression. Cousin checking in. deriding word to dare as none. Appropriated for having tunes. personnels of here and through. Pains of a saving place. healing ambience with likely inference. Nothing telling an understanding. Cracking the memory. Prick with greatness. modesty of the discourtesy. Slum suppression of detached sailing. top small vessels with oceanic norms. Require great currents with pleasure romps. Deferment of retirement. Seek a relief of absconscion. state of padded retention, deigned with health patches and massages. indulge obsessed loves of their eccentric proofs. queenly things of welling the depths. guarding non weighed. regains by filtered pips, dark with rocky associates. millions of years. professions of new ones and young ones. crustaceans of appetites, profoundly seasoned with exclamations. littering insects of topical relevance, high with cool mischance. watching prance of daily attendance. rich welter of hell dispelled, leak habit for hoping. coy with survival leads and using Darwin. secular mauves of drink in colours. learn the locus on banter plaster. small hand of using reprimand. status of acquired abuse. status of increasing in misuse. getting away with vibes. being knowing how to. Admission as philosophical with the end result. angry within curiosity about what trumps. each appointee vetted for being. close brush with mistrust. resented after elations. what's what. magnificence of blood in drenching. posts of surgeons and slay men. in the thick of having done. daily suffrage of punch and run again. British bulldogs to thistles and bees. pollinate dollish norms. let things pass. touch horrors till horrors are lunch forecasts. break of head in stubbornness. brutish mute. qualm from steeping. storing shiver attendance. wondering on the awfulness of escape. to be shared of the burden. Curbed with less enthusiasm.

22

Paragraph psh

Luxuriantly by luring requester. Is anyone on their own. Front fetch over. volunteer. Due to plasma there's fauvism. Hoarse supplant expectancy, thus suffuse. Match of swatch. Back seat pipe a change of socks. Orbit quit compliment. Garnet poke former. find of no source. Incest of invention. task In fluency. Of a sigh in truancy. Abrupt run hypothetic fun. Gas in the room. its what I left. Insensible calm return theft. Wrecks how it was. Sprint clause due. Sin jet religion. Subtle back shout. Hunger brink a rim. Kind on blank.. find on passing. Indicate by plea. Crank dined. Light expectation. Deep too flat. Brag that found around. Inebriate basking. Innumerable shy provision. Pliancy and willing plates. Truancy of dance, participant suit. Duplication of desert. Favoured not hurt. Blank occupancy fully ordered. Gaze supplant the potted maze. Oh happy tree that grand the mother fondly. fix coursed the fascinated number. All and Sundry from support. lessen why an acorn spot. Stamp that slot. Make ague of provision. Woe become the true condition. Ditch a lane in flow. Seed on rejoinder; need for supplement. Plunge runs innocence. Reads right. despotic ode. Innovated counter. crown a noun. Grand correct at might. Handed out excite. White harvest. Piss and restraint, faintly crook a fencer. Who spoke. None that owed a pleasant Lord. Mistaken truer comprehension. Correct at verse of satan's tension. Phrase that sat beside the freeze and curled to hit the hitler peas. by pod invent the torrid haunt. Nod invent hooter. Pray seem the same. Applaud compliant looter, such as it wonder. Comment part of mockument. Worzel postcard. Vetting a variant let that catch upon a license yet. Message snag meant. Think it only intermission. Perch in company. High mind Yet not. Divisible in divisible load. Risible invisible showed. Display at lenience. Endowed of sex of texture sense. Shy provoke a blanket sack. Choice of core in variance. Stoop Warrant. Pass and name an Arian. Skip a stroll that pluck in luck to be. to be Toby. Wit without aid. Peut etre feller. Fever a measure extent. dismay without recourse. Of body to preserve a force. Worship made. Fine thread thatch a patch. Time in a real prison. Watch countenance. Wow congruent. now suit errant. Cloud cleanser mixture. Thunder smaller head. Emphatic lead a pseud, clumsy clamber over thin. Fatal sound attraction sin. Choler by ancient sated route. Gum that poke the miser mute. Warm. In swarm the belling. Want for the everlasting. My friend is dying. My friend has died. President commend; aside. Prick they fall. Prick they fell. One of each beside the wall. Infuse righteous boot. Keep At bay. Station shortly cross the file. Only cross to fill Sight. my light my serve. Humilities mouse preserve. Verify me vengeance, me ignored. Insufficient injured code. Over No cowing; sorry. Long stop not worry. Resolution lot resolution. Theft the widow that left. Double bass. Mended a worse impermanence. Snap at strange and veto change. Keep the fit. Suck a skeptic. Of any man thus the afternoon. That my cast which is my set. That my hate. of silence inset. Way in gain and against. Whistle quote. Inglorious bastard; place. share miss that scare. crude to bear. Dole out dominion. Beneath of not. excessive fuck. Beneath of use. perceptive bark. Race that crane. Implausible gain. Fuss clause. Permissive of the fine; reverse. Wobble in syrup. hem. Fine to pick on. me. Sorry pay to be in work. Impediment revolve a wake up. perk. Thoughtfulness for blanking. Spoken not. Thoughtfulness to shun. Thought for blanking come. Insufficient order, some in none. Advantage of advantage. bake predator. Spam want ham and ham. Through made piece; one in concept made a fleece. Alliterated choice. Against sun which heard its voice. Minion of a mondial spoon. Poleaxe food oft lava loon. Appointed court. set the soon. Day favoured intern. Drum hum drum done, puppet past copse of patience. Skin scale wrap. Move home alone off public moon. What snot the charm. Intermediable thing. Hang purse, subtly curse. Pan retrieval evaluate. Neuter childless. Perfect childer childer. Nuff of commitment. cover. meaning lapse collapse. Proper leave crowder. repair over. Further orgy. lease of paper. Due at light. suppliant beat start about bite. Stage upon reluctance. be corrected. White public property resound the night. Asleep which rail. mess clamp. Fuck tramp. Clam raise the instance to ban. Further most which harbour from. Rumble crumble ready prow, proclivity roam. Amount mount. an ounce and province. Orgy lease paper. Shift at short shrift. Thrift. Funny make bod. bow Mood pull plough. Tear chart. Honey import. Train view educant. Bend round Shakespeare. Slang verify legacy. Load apparent rake. Man of a flea. ton on a bumper. carriage. Speak no English, English speak. Can I squeeze past. What has hurt has not explored. Express and disperse not the surplus. Council by dream impart the column. Iron by crowding. Juxtapose by orient arrest. Development of culture rest. Mean average expectance; manage. They had no idea I had bosoms. Pneumonic leisure. warm. excess through verve; sworn. Infringement instruct binge. Captivate by kidnap creep. None of them are orphans. They don't gob. Job. Omnipotent sufficiency fore. Fire upon cause. to rise expertise. Withdraw by instance, surfeit sleep. Work companion keep. Vibrancy meek. no fever. Follow selfish fault. equal vault profess dumb. disarm. Rap about equal guess. Stance resolve stress. Strong remove. Group regroup by self instalment. Louvre.

23

Late Winter

Malvolio to the action, papered accomplished, intended. bread rolled in movement is not sanctioned on vocality. instruction subsidy other than tragedy by oblivion. See sharp instrument, catch the art sight. Lifting page does a shake of the head. Sitter can infuriate. Pause for thought relative to inaction. Storage condense dance fruit in a nut cracker. Deliverance to feeling bowed to pick up an arrow. second applause seizure melancholy. Laws or a gym tuck. Bic fine compound scary nobleman. Impossible scrawl with feeling stub from bookie draw. Nib from Smiths and not Mont Blanc. Tools and craftsmanship stave hearty plans for precedent laws. ruler and curver, ninety degrees and line without joint, Amen. Hand line down to the right, down to the left, more creased in clench than stroke. It says haughty wits are conjugated to the verb of bile consequence. action given to a nail. Pull me up the stairs mother, pot of gold in sex. Enquiries and assistance start from here, the institute of clause. Arm raise question, leg the trample. Swinging and climbing raise the temple. Hating job a tireless exercise. undone shop management for standing, writing, talking, watching for keeping warm. Many folk in bright jackets marshaling. Contrary destruct as it means to defend. positive curse on strain inhibition. Robert De Niro in the library with a fist at his cheek. Object piled up according to flatness and gravity. Circuses do this with spring but generally pages are records. LPs stack in rows alphabetical to mood. Abba Zebedee coin Calas on variants of seventeen ninety nine. Get the Gazette for local affairs, walks and some invention. danger room. shampoo forgotten left behind. Fulham Palace Road brow band. Horse for bridle necessary. Consider information just in. man parable girth. Follow hide a warm leather coat. Skin mend wearing patch. Cotton prefer light sour argument. yet converse. up worth seed to patrol. Vigilance crave passion. Pepper chalk score boredom. Imbue good subject. Luxury tongue trolley off to ink or excuse me. Psychopath at large wear bracelet in gut. Quilt pasta with aubergine sauce. Presume cousins for problems. Preserve low cause to harmful ways. sake of insurgence digestive news, rabbit encircled by sense. penitent badger, quarry minded eagle. grace and vulgarity suit velvet lilt. Wildlife program. Search cross patches. sight line for gunning down pestilence through participation. glorious moment upon rampage. Shake in comparison for donation. Summer day secure shine. Black fruited hedgerow, absolutely close range colour and thorn. Dickensian rain Get past. a big issue. down and out on the climb. Some carry on about fish. Carrier bag paper do. House of Fraser, warrior in faith of colour. Red yellow lorry crinkle pebble shaky tree catch cranky. Fright neurosis make the point of canvas. legume potage and fifty. recycle the loo. valued point in shilling may be useful, may be contrite. Perambulate stick point shop on St. Martin's Lane. Half a minuscule discussion hangs about. fingers caught in street on top. spare minutes of transgression. Whether the bag is a babe. Bag is grainy, bag unfolds. Bag winter marshal tin, bag pepsi coke and gin. Challenge of lozenge suck good egg. Passing soda, weeping bed. lady says I made it here. Squares battle pose with bleeding torch. old bag cook new potatoes. Well. Given the time of day. time shuffle an old pogo and Lang Syne. Bag infinite drag waylaid. Dame Edna storm stage, Norman drop name left right centre. Volcano blubber lava scary nose bleed. People shouldn't be picked. lava's no good for sledging. nick on neck from gangrene unpleasant and retarded. People making pots of money, splosh. Takeover bid steal price. Funny old friend with spy glass. Lance Romantic business deal. Auctioneer plain bag shopping. Looping OCD. Can't remember country member. Anatomy program Skin. Tissue. page take its clothes off. Flay skin of St. Bartholomew. Sistine Chapel Blancmange brain. side speech back vision. Front personality motor. cerebellum smoke alarm. rim, medulla, corpus colosseum, basal. The Fly with Geoff Goldblum. Inanimate object. inside out grey tie. dear Pokahontas foetus. Gillie has been an old dog for many years. X ray radiation. Robert Burns day. Turandot Lucozade. Office Angel, Second hand minute. hour minute, second and hour compact extend. got there get. against clock the digital Strap. wrist mantle hinge balance, hook nail, neon all category. X figment Y reality 2 arms 1 leg 1 legs 1 arm 3 - 6 scissors without thumbholes. Tooth nail stick plaque. stock ladder tap reminder. Toxic, no such thing (as a complete revolution). Spiral coil wave, biological magnification enlarge image. DNA strand loop. Split and two strands tangle. One strand loop. Step and pond, noose and chain. Cappuccino, Cistercian, Franciscan. Donkey Kong II. Monkey or ape. Copy sound like Bear bating. baton press. animal conflicts are multiplied. Cumbersome stone of irrelevance. Texture furnish shop. much too good saddens off. Chance crack at linguistic taste. Smart Alec delivers cut. Time kiss goodbye and then on its way. as opposed to badge granting requests. Dole and remedy by purveyor. Fine wine fun time. Purveyor of cheese for a smile. Purveyor MacDonald when Donald is old enough Mac to understand burger nutrition leaving things open ended like a good deck position exploded. Whatever. Pass and fail on the same day, fail then pass. Fail see how to set test. start again. Pass obliviously should that fail. Newcomer clear perception, doubt disability, inability and choice legendary. The great thing to remember is the greatest thing about. Look on wonder. Know how to look and switch off may forfeit a program, holiday or explanation. What nose nose what, Cicada, Vosene, Sport eye one son Drops Eye. Ayurvedic plastic surgery, Dope in the ear, rolling joint. always watching prices, One fine day, Agatha Christie, pheasant Scoff one bullet, impatient Jacqueline, Toby jug, ostrich and pear buff, Cluedo plenty, Axiom darn, nail 'moins cuit', Adrian Lukis, Rail Land, Drain Dr Denial, Sari UK Slim, Bryan Adams, Duck Luck, Skull Kulin, Dali Kiss Nurd. Secrecy one, privacy two, ownership three, expression four. Cathedral Not as bad as murderous good inventive. North should, south could, east would, west do. This way! Drawing East north a cross to stand. men who want go north of crickets. difference between poach cross section, scotch cut. Pan white yolk, breadcrumbs pork, white, yolk, usually cold. Inferiority complex manifest by

A Questioning, loud claims, higher thought speech volume ration.

B Carry on regardless. Body language word, speech literature, jaw drop, AB interchangeable. Somebody called Mia. Not much known, but destiny sewn. Attention sit still, no smoking home, Perform procession Calculator solar powered battery. work day and night, light in electric. Dictator sleep, thinker awake, example smoke. Manner broke, professional airs, graces Sport Scrum, victory, tackle, sacrifice. Reward take spent spirit helicopter, air bus, airplane. Ecstasy in silk dressing, pajama nude nightie. Net size millionaire to marlin, shrimp, Audi chain hoops. A1 Write in black and white, charge. detective X kills Y and believes in him X kills Y's children cry X become followers of X Y isn't there. What's the answer. Who should it belong to. Opinion witness spell. Messiah Hessian, Jesus, Bishop Posh, Clergy Jericho, Friend Nothing, Master Horoscope, Aquarius Preach. Tessa Jowell is confusing. Subtitle time delay. Lenny Henry Disabled Lavender, simple rose equal room. St Paul know not what. turn away private to public convenience. Mr Nobody plays chord leather satchel, scarf about neck. humble jumper stroll by perspex head stop moderately far from wife with good reason divorce totty line bordering style of book strategy of musical lover preciously choosing Ian McEwan as someone contemporary so it couldn't be helped. Music dreadful jumping at the symbol, spot line, trill quaver, Joni Mitchell on a bongo. Bitch getaway, chicken cherry hook line sink. juice plenty saliva dentist. Cleverly scrape flakes of gum look blood dish done. Nobody with a string flossing denture models. emergency cocktail, Japanese food, Mountbatten dial spring itinery. Didn't wear hat today, didn't face the north, stood astride, turned and jumped a pond, chin face down. quiet on the way, disco line approach with jazz pretty ladies, censure. Feet stick again suggestion bring on usual cues over the bridge perhaps, a snack there, fact timing steady for drain. keeper sit stop before hand. poise after stance when before should have stood the ground of double. O. Child meets enfant enface sans trace, sauve que moi. Dance in greenie trance, hop to right of way. bag message man with every little helps. Turn heel on exit face. living dead print across lines facing west, straighter and more blest for this reward is holiday. Aboard cruise ship fantastic move bombastic, arch remedy on compass fake perfume for solitude bleed to worm. Crucial perm evidence dance of obvious pleasant condition ripen old fruition, eat scratch custard meter blue corn both syllable and remedy. Choose vents, bargain for air conditioning. Walk idle away chalk on cheese so promising at worst purse gather on wheels and look who turns up least protracted tame invested. Scurry a long crack at heel brushing up carving steel meddling and posture now a saint. now live on curfew of event. singular most good time teddy boasts, glass fix eyes just when things begin to feel.

Le gendarme Jean Val Jean. Il veut mourire, dying and laughing the same et qui s'appelle la nome sourire dans la chaise a cote en bas. action stare to dine upon the snow though it drinks not and is made of steel pins and needles on toes.

24

Settlement to the intrigue, waste doctrines of doing to persevere with notch harms, pegging the goals of infinite wrongs. strange puzzles of being done to, braking Go set for start offs, setting darlings of ready to bang, mood hinge harbour. At the little companions. signature tunes of mint interpreters, shares of war declarations shingling relevance of small incidents, bulging frisson of extortion with deaf cares none hung. dismissive times table associates of shoving the testament, this mine to this tie, sick as poorly numb with inches of progression, even cousin checking in, deride word dare as none, appropriated for having tunes, personnels here through. jocular pains of saving place, healing ambience with likely inference. nothingness of telling the understanding, cracking memory prick with greatness, a modesty of discourtesy. slum suppression of detached sailing, top small vessel with oceanic norms, requiring great currents with pleasure romps, suck deferment of retirement, seek hole relief abscond, state of padded retention, deigned with health patches and massages, indulging in the obsessed loves of eccentric proofs. queenly things of welling the depths, guarding the non weighed regains of filtered pips, dark with rocky associates of millions of years. professions of new ones and youngs, crustaceans of table appetites, profoundly seasoned with exclamations, litter insects of topical relevance, high with cool mischance, neither apologetic for watch dumb prance of daily attendance. rich welter of hell is dumbest to most dispelled, leak habit for hoping, being coy with survival leads and using Darwin. secular mauves of drinking the colours, learning on locus banter of warred plaster. small hand of using reprimand, the status of acquired abuse, status of increasing misuse, getting away with lurid vibes, knowing admission, philosophical end result. angry curiosity about what trumps, he angry and the fear, each appointee being vetted for being copious with close brush, either at the head with curious mistrust, resented after elations. magnificence of blood drenching, curious posts of surgeons and slay men, the thick of having done. daily suffragette of punch and run again, British bulldogs to thistles and bees, pollinate dollish norms to let things pass, touching the horrors till horrors are lunch forecasts with breaks of heads and stubbornness. brutish impolity of being mute, having qualms with steeping in. proper attendance of storing shiver, wondering on the awfulness of escape, assuming black heads of incrimination, relieving to be shared of the burden. blithe with language improbity, counter achievements of goal initiatives. ridiculous underscore of shame to man's more, being the absolute Goliath. river crossing of stone throwing, whimpering chameleon craving cuddles and muddles with flashy flavour, brew brides of hologram rains. boots and fashions of restrain distorted, distorted, always setting up proper conductor, winning elected interloper to present a prize of instruction size, plead to mask the hopeless cause. Brilliance of small things irrelevance brings, only sulkiness on unfairness and sustaining incredulity. exception to the ties of humanity, super worms of subtle sobriety, being level to iced cakes with things that weren't but proved mistakes. proper tuning times, mattering fork lifts and food rates with humble position. mask of enormous pastes, glutton with thank you probes. Only sense of prompt. slip creams of seriously green, chug and batter thump, pave with laymen slabs, jeer on representatives. appoint gloves and reprieve ordinary stakes of prejudice. Confound extremes. tidal matter of healthy headlines, swish sides of involved clatter, attend with dismay. agenda of struggle's belter, feed on mini buns of normal systems, seek in on squared steps of that harm to this extension. teased with grumpy reasons as if grumpy attend an adjective. un described use of sharing out core truce, always magnanimous, inspired. Scatter fear in copious presence, manifold fires of disconcerted, walk about peaceful, heat disarray and infect a warm home. Possession with title inflation, scold observation action, plough muds up with statements to grow, bean to Jack sprout, tallness with labour's microscope. joke out when chemistry sets. guardian of Perspex, glazed plastic class of scratch pulse, pause to select the herb, turn off word curb, gutter fresh for rich with real fondness for rubbish and jettison. throwaway cradling victim, one proper honesty of surrender. Defiant plumes of onward exhumes, bewilder given with abstinence, suck invective of depravity, will closure sincerity, postpone loves for improved decency. composure of dawning custom, find no revel with blame but overtake. quartz of mischief sorry flake, unwelcome counter for crying departure. strange impetuous bursts from walkabout cherubs of miniature might. Grown wards of jury lords, inexperience petals of childish mettle, mean with poses of understanding, communions with memory permanence. wilts of soulful Giants. Enormous flare going nowhere, importance offer unseen risks. Shell counterfeits of excuse. pass buck, phrase employ to board truck. heavy see the reeds. whistle tunes invite options, cull happiness as nowhere exertions. None of the company suit tyranny, only opinions. lurid case of proper alerts, unknown to capital forts, ascension statistic, deliberate each skirt. possibly this. Holbein nun of muddling fun, boredom of high art with relocation chart. assume other house will borrow anything for a friendly arrow. Life in vixen fixture, wait for ducklings and grizzly bears. together party notoriety, answerable society, pleasantly housed with roving disparity. subservient story only in been there. Empty chin misgivings, resilient and omnipotent, settled with douse dipped sheep, tick off to shag again on latest fawn. Employ wolf. command later years of discharge, whim of bellicose vitriol compare later with fine and dandy over supper. Foresight disclose nutter, ransom of keeping ahead. Great trip moon, qualified with pop and ballad. mystery palm of drawing rains, boulders for horizontal characters. Declare fight in passing, un propose place exchange proceedure. Luck park smart, soothed hitch. improper voice of imitation, unheard falter of word choice, no speech but to mimic again, subtle reproach of Amen. Prayer to revive lives again, expose to use re gathering. Fold course of settlement norse, onward to inhabited dwelling. constant extension of dousing the heat, all coals to stoking retreat, hiding and regaining with the bound craving, not understanding the setback for being obtuse. knowing loops traumatic roots, tripping toasts of passers by, causing shivers and curious pelters, why mean carefree. Proper trajectory of let me in, occasioning idleness with flowing rims, taking there route of most astute, all bedded with seeping. Slightly ordinary pretense of social disgrace, having a lot to answer for, having saved none. Required tries of having overcome, at best with furnishing the room, employed to indulge in being lifted. charms of serious mischance, such are the chasms. Display void to waling abroad, being gawped for crossing reasons. echoes and shouts of beckon perversions, wondering about pet dogs and assertiveness. Belongings and divisions to coax the extensions, being normals to set apart stencils. spray patterns of recognitions, toying with former positions, gleaning quest for letting up, wondering where everyone lives and stealing hope. stains of lost fears, resolute with precious smart, glove temporary job, then fingered to sell on. Tenuous nerves of being put upon, straining the gallant surveillance with reinstative-ness, call crowd of dismissed pride, pointed at for brief spats, dotted words to dung, caning overseers with improper suffering for something living. Microbe and germ of testament, hungered for and rejected. toughness of resilience, a more worthy pre ponder-ence, for happiness has a pause, where vanity finds slush and rudeness, where encouragement has a false flush. saving face of secretiveness, unknown to depleted gong. witness with cowardice, accomplis mask, follow examples required past, measure had to be taken. Mean standing ovation, whip cracked with disability. Best advice address inconsistency, finding best reason with simplicity. here comes sophistication, right and left hand retention, choosing sounds for verbal extortion, whittling sanity with please inflict. cast place of garb inter fact. Set plaid horn the charge. luxurious with dextrous large, sized with left over complicity. Attend luminous emergence, proper convergence of rescue. hinge of being blind, opened and shut bound, supple complexion of having been painted, manage assume favour from injected implement. part acceleration, chance to set loose. temperamental misuse leveling crime, beholder share design. proper misery of observing court, presuming fun between rinses. supposed of improved that doctors stepped in. qualified tones of setting art, mischievous with finding out. robot plait weave likeness, expect and hang up to pass on and heel. two inches from somewhere before. thank require light darkness, shaded with a health improvement, spirit of joy windproof buoy, thankless terminal play, right as warm display. best safen tuck, curious belief of puckered, fairy parts of slavish waters, require examination all the time. Least harm to anyone, pulling time of rode upon. Tend horse as wild beast, set rein settle increase, evolve magnitude to tamed lies, douse callous expanse with calls on pride. Ridicule peck best described, tough another side. Silly whim pathetic grin, insistence of place and fear together. want backs of lost cheer, fluffy chits of noble rear. insistence neare pave, summary times of grave. Subject account for daily despairs, resign perverted dominance. sleep pews of plundered troves, bookish inherited woes, sincerity with emotional frugality, afraid of suggestions. It was evolved possession, relinquished norms of foreign reflection, teased with greatness and mints of achievement, priced with ballots of other powers. wanted by ambition, courted with nations intentions. Dream worth politicians, scorned for the cost. Level headedness settling up, the access mould of touching stuff. moon cakes of assembled Crufts, dogs courting to prissy bells and coats in Paris. Memory and descriptive, unsaid nods of wonder permissive, actual with elementary pings, each ointment of news about ordinary form. Fascination counter down, eavesdrop day to day in gown. Bladder pressure drawing times faults. Listen high prescription, useless quality jettison totality, figure. Attend thought bless use, margin glue mark up. Wring hands of reading laws, mucky condense the paragraphs. Involve language of disgust with value, prominent breaking down. Speak horns but noise of extreme and fun times at fairs. Melt rite of good relief, get better view. Juxtapose carry through, joyous bells. Trees and fells, landscapes of pressures. Hail falls to angle claws, disappoint probation with summons reinstated, unholiness to fortress goddess, looks in poisoned waters. Frozen spits of remonstrance, insist with ifs that a gilt edge stagnates. Prang with appointed wondering, dirty underwear of living in the hall. readable sense that horror requites, called upon by ravenous truths own downfall. buttery pictures of confession, inscribed without attention, deficit of extension, howling after pose. What thing in store, chomp acquired waste. Tuck in to Friar's chin, layers of blubber harpoon. Immediately bathroom, breaths to laughing wreathes of rolls. Pearls doing butchers, digested tracts of energy literatures. Pretty thongs of beauteous pawns, nonsense with going wrong. Breakfast for dinner, freshness for villains. statues of incisors, welling plunge from catering produce. At length beast left, kennel protect pup. babe go to sleep, alone chain of peaceful sound. safety good hound, bowl before chase. Scratch days frustrated, acquire love before deserted. removed from walking with, walled and barred to pace protected, unfairly shut effectiveness, minding warn. Minute turn to do, deposit disperse. shovel. Leash strained cord, retun gait of master flawed. no chance with seems to wear, coat with shampoo or soggy hair, condition and habitation, depended upon to drop at will. Dog nine and five, worker man constant hive. Some requirements are gut reactions, marveled with restraint and forbidden. Swears of oaths and adulates, exchange views of respect. Draw past and wish to pet, escape exceed to spare affection. wealth of gosh and making puppies, dog collar returns. People and core learns, nesting flights with more perms, styling hair to sealing baldness, hungry for youth and ports. Tiger drop earlier prevention. Appease risky flop of precarious teddy, clearly on the brink of demise. turn to retrieve sorry had to achieve. Hunt after soft braziers and feathers in terms of lurex shorts. molt yearns of wanting brushes, funny dolls requiring dressers. Some dogs appreciate sound importance, making friends all over the place, other dogs learn the mistake of dropping ash instead of good turns. Simile in friend, appreciating a manufactured sense for music. Feedback with swimming groups on the free vibe. Very little advancement to the piper's tune, gaining for the lure of entertainment, a constant spectacle. Tee total ness of finishing the bottle, wondering hat became of the pout. licentiousness of wearing bootees and borrowing hairbands. acceptance of tribe, defining insurgency with later whispers to the noise police. mess of beat and quality, beams for low roves, acquitting assembly to set new page ahead. blank exposure to sensation, clubbed with value. Idealist hound darkness with celebration, drying trousers and then perspiring. Clean groom of appeal to everyone, net time for covetous indulgence with farm. Make up rosy infusion, none of the education, speaker mend plying house with notes. all round beauty of nothing to look at. Only good recipients, marble fringed with lashes and stow aways. memory invokes speech, a debate on enhancing clothes and frillies where cream buns used to be obvious. Infusions with sound inclusions, agreeing to reconvene the taste. Vault of having time, boots and coat hangers of wardrobes with number retrieves to chart nits, twanged from angelicus. Poise of hearing to purchase, uncommented to relax and bathe. Tension reprieves the rest of the world, at large with out . Mediocrity to access, make FUMBLE the revolution, let Minatore be the study, fitted to the moral in pure form. Slope of required jest, warm house of in barbarous trace. Large bulge of coat, impetuous prince of show this snort. At the helm of amphetamine, heroine of leaning improbability. Thirst of barging consequence for a true surreality. Holiday to the hot spot, the proper cleanse of danger, travel being the mileage of freshness, temporarily. Learn of an extensive wardrobe, crease exactions of being bare, animal sector. Candidate prime minister, flight take a prejudice. Creeping roles of croons, very rarely and exotically obvious. Realms of obvious indulgence, prevented on, pause for greed, delay has juncture. Pest request for straining crane, common of stately. Prevention, assign Reliance van. Mistrust lack of serious forecast, mock level hood with meeting breakdown. Insistent swerve the nerve, copping out with proper horn, shoes for speaking on whose behalf. Retreats of flowers and vessels, boomeranging portals with snack retorts to stave off. Any sugared outburst, any treat and wrapper outface, embezzled with occasional glutton, relinquished with obvious disgusting. Primal gorge with margarine spread, conceding with the hopping list not to butter the potatoes persevering deadly with smoking habit contingencies, wondering change from Bensons, saying beat up name of the brand, Marlboro demand stone circle, hen weird attend. disprove the admin state. At once surreal disgrace, boarding hip with interface, surprising bursts of wind, embattling Lillette trim, test sphincter of Nile pavilion, saying cricket for pads and bowlers. Onward prance look askance, size dress up fast, concede past to daring starch on common place of drag tobacco. pomposity use unelected expertise, library wards of leathered books, hustle see perfect brain. Insight of remarkable gains, extended from prying fleas make worthy mites patrons, hunger investigative doctrines.

Ordinary route acquiring clout, none jewels and bibles allowed cow, only necklace grazing beasts, milking Heidi in her storybook. Beckon return to excellence form, troop colour with partridge sightings, idiotic pheasant crossings where sights of dumb squirrels appease worries. proper omen of gnome in garden, crows of nesting lightnings. animals in kingdom with their god spake. Live and let give squashing fighting. Face wear conjugate pair. gesture remark made bed. Hapless tirade restate. Helter skelter horse malleable divorce, living legs of humans have vibrant skies of frequent generations. Mice and gerbils, weeks to week with mystic hurdles. great great great great greet great great great grandmother of Fluffy the frosty hamster. Week to week purge hurdling alabaster, chirrup incessant coast with prescribed laps because land meets. Waves of cigarette comments, relax with sandy wear down. Golf drive brand in holing court serial stand, adjust swing of flags in breezes, outdoor conducive boldness, requite light bluster gaining. Calmness present tense, hurrying backward gone, hearing sincerity with give in mark of laughing endoscopy, whatever that is. silver crust of chance deceive, pass on certainty that fashions change. Once upon a time bakery purge again, habit skin rabbit early morning, though peasants are well fed. Sport kings jests at misgivings, owing grudge temperance of land mines. serious thwart for beautiful escort, apparent route of deport. house of extinguishing like, played recently crow's tate, thank for famously sank, flew land to journey lend. Disappeared sunk with bread in soup, discussed and weather blamed. Mysteries of giving up magnitude, greet washed up containers and famously smooth. Scottish grouse whisky perverse, where did it swore and remembered. level incapacity and violence incredulity, haunted dextrous incongruity, sleeving shine to abnormal designs, hopping foot of a bruised ego wondering out of the jail with hangover recovery. Annadin free chemist, absolving witness to equally spent. Who match bottle to bottle. Who malty throttle. Sent hazard suffering ballad, poor wretch of was discovered. Seek medal extreme survival, only meet canyon retrieval, gore full of bones from outsized stone, sealed to lava of Pompeii's quarter, blast censure to archaeological trigger, completely clean face to histrionic wonder. Infusion to book for a page, lesson Romans lived. Teach innocent thunders, progressive use move on to PE. Juncture saved by bell, rest plush with time tell, refurbished for current tunes and radio moons, dictated on room everywhere signs and the chance not to sneer. Equipment help obvious kelp, glean for wild seals and puffins. Safety notch of imbue passions kept with air bubbles for resilience. Who's Who depth insistence, decline submarines. Lookout carts of Frankie Howard, comedy sections of Carry On questions. Mirth bellicose girth betraying ladders, jeers at old prodigiousness. Sanctity wasted verdures where wind and guts have given up. Excelsior of glorious senate, mown down with fates, reminisce toy sailors, wobbled from leagues and features. Require proverbial pelter soothe youthful exterior, finding dalliance a purpose to keep fit, finding the what for for a geriatric. Reason is there to succumb scare, say chill in the wind for propping the bar. Invite open again, backing off disastrous plaster, move on! Presence of invites comparison states, her's to Henry VIIIth jokes. Appalling laughs to wives in plaster cast, unparalleled accomplishment of dissolution. Jets and spraying extremes of countryside dismantling. Chaos crooks of precious routes, pewter with driving speeds as disposable cups of polystyrene. Creeping forms of comparison gongs, updating principle from canon to bulletin. Escalated surge of rubbish to re emerge, a state gift to accept the stool, Landmark Sofas to Doritos. Wash away lives of educating Ritas, lingua franca professor. Risk and sex embezzle flex of human interpreters. Brilliance detractors, scened with polluting exactors, getting old men to turn in their graves. please don't put me there! Funniest patrolling Alsatians, see what the dog thinks. learning retractor with staving the martyr, keep sweetness of pastries as things to enjoy. Dentures protrude adventures, unblemished robot with bleeps and fittings. Fashion old school, audience of ruling wisdoms. Atmosphere of incisive petitions, gathering in on doubts of parsons. goodly trait of serious bate, something sex does to appease vixens. laughs on animal probations likening greatest cowards in history. unwritten time of Godzilla's restrain, the way it just bulges up on equator every day. Be diamond! Stone sets seizure, glassiest stare. Presume niceness to settle down prices, encourage stale man to earn. rage of worry to find nobody, prodding slug with a stick. Thickness width of crust, prejudice with smells to typing accuracy. fingers have their own touches, armed and booted with relaxations. Dress down inflated bun, reach extinguish at the end of a candle meal. Thin and thorn again, S shape change lane. angry beast inviting demon, goad suggestion with curb less enthusiasm. week with hilarity, poked to dance. week left to stop the gap, relay gorge food fight. bedlam screen to being cream pie. Laugh direction, serious of snake's eye. Temptation set up and withdraw, belly dancing steaks' underscore. cobra spit match, final scene struck to scratch. Lines of teams of goodly keens, inspired slates of incubates. Disabled with doings to tiny moanings, tongued with poetry to commentary, pricking busy involvements of fisty cuffs. dizzy making slurs of serious improvisers, wounded every day with prominent overlay. Floor go betweening, goading tech repeating to start again. Every race with criminal inter fact, every mace prescribed with sparks. Pantomime pans of glittering positions, fuming tans of sensible cookery. Cold and inhospitable kitchen with plans for seduction, eating out of the qualified rut, employed to consume. Minion answer oblivion, having no orders to carry out, only conceive with hithering. What are companies with club proclivities, understandings of blocked discrepancies. Simple Paul may not jump, and simple simon may not hump. Inheritance guide omnipotence with prevention, as serfs to dictator's opprobrium. Tin scalp mettle fuzz, conclude forthright avarice. Though youths require their troves, paths warn parental overthrows. Poor consistency with curfew discrepancy, keep out of the street. Set back quaich of perceived truth, paving roads as first commuters. Sense of order number, numb love, bursting with logic and lottery ticket. spent entire fortune, sidelined emerging nation. Sultan of woman, self contained harem, next quest motherhood twaddle. At once rejection was qualified exaction, removed sphere of bouncy section of coordinate caption, after note of margin heads. Last spit packet, wisp to a wing maggot. An engorged bin of giving again, recognizing outcast flame, for it has no home. Only time expires with fortune's fires, as long as there is a picnic place. Construct verbal aqueduct, reduce comment rocky outcrop. Weave name feed, conclusion should be dressed. Postpone love as bargain vest, kept warm without a coat, honoured for a safe tote. Beast race to generate, whip fast jockey advocate. This one seriously too large to barge with obvious sport, content instead to sow winnings, drop people with hiatus for their safety. Melodrama apish quiver, entrusting zoo to take sides. pens and wardens, abstention of insults, space short for kangaroo bounce. No proper road for Herod's fairies. consumption baby gazzumption. Property winds of bad news. permission vans of playful orangutans, wouldn't drive for cute rescue. Absolved place of the axis face, being kept in the dim north. Excellence of questioned birth, as unsure to secret mirth, owing true kindness to lost observance, forgive continued examination and tag a goose flight. Feathers return colour to learn, define body of shiver's nativity, goose bumps to bald arms, describe hairless things as cradled swans, trips to Nuneaton. Drugs n Pining for love and a hand of instruction. true glory trust's dominion. Hero whet for appetite assassinate words. Dim bulb assurance sties, affect cheer to crimp hope leap, make fingers of woods to belong. Walk among the secret forest. Drop saps of habit loll it, infuse the sunk boast of dare to choose. Time fancy take up stretch, concede match fetch, share pavilion of think but a weight of ton. Appease verse, scroll up light pert. trail of inference on the day's delinquency, set next troop of tick tock stoop. Shrill quiet overhaul, complain sizes of guessing. Kill things of the single man, blended in margarine. First with stirs and feet, second cut guts of lots of bowels, thirdly, just to shape the try well. Thirst shared things of concession game what brings. Steadily encroaching ways of question books to carrying trays. Muddled pockets of mystery sockets, saying shame was worthy, curious affectation. Why should shame be consequence of looking at when, seething on the past, fate of wrong turn. Goodly proceeds everyone's nurse, notch up wild purse, fame bang with ring out am. afternoon with stamp pots. Perhaps thing there to fuddle, but interestingness is how to cuddle. Each surrender, less stressed with most, leaving the care wavy, prone to a call autumn brown, dispensing worth from after noun. Fullness relieving pain, expecting let off entertain, wider understanding. Accepted use of flicking puce, seeing if cheek greens or gets indented with touch, flooded beings of moment such, bottoms of word fuzz aways, thronging insertions with low exactlies. Colloquial things towns, twinned with Swiss villages, appealing hedges and cats, simply incomprehensible sign. Pounced upon wrong, hooray to slavery, wonderful thing of hiding amongst thieves. Cluttered heads of mental fellers, all growing up to plan proper parties with baroque masterpieces where wallies feel at home. Set up announced, set part will display ounce, parrot place to carp, settlements with work. Working free lance amongst blizzard fence, determining expiry to high pressures of inquiry, all importance! Dipping amongst the choices for breaks to furnishings, being gluttonous to the risk of cigarettes at tea, and no to standing slightly. Increasing value of livid to tell you, pushing open gate to let the pigs run on. Around bend furthering mend, honing sanity stand of livery. questioned shapes of healing states, setting proper suggestions of fear to jelly torture where lost is queer and where prongs scrape on annihilation, surveyed amongst close shave. Role ports of soothed warts, decency respect jitter bus, make talk downs with grand hogs, prescient to speech when whirrs are ricocheted. Having a brain of a fan, rotate lob clam, having say so there am, routing plight on forearm, making up take, copious remove. Take over at helm, calling decent citizens to join in, pend sense of madness until foolish ravages of risk embalm. Self assessment is toying calm, embarrassed as ambitious plight. sonorous would of in sight, having teeth with jaws, chosen for being capped with gold. fair hold of storing loft, retiring dreams and horrors with games rooms and rafters, magnificence of cruel paintings, banquets and lost swimmers, grasping life against slow motion. Empowerment requires promotion, a certificate with redemption, something with the medley grasp where spoof sets out appropriately dressed. Claim to masking ordinary graft, closest resemblance toilet apologies, being meek to loss ness of washing hands, always slinking in and bunged with what was that for. funny glues of pressed seals, emerging from pressed palms, oozing in clear blobs, expecting tissues and stand backs. Temples waling through unshaken to grueling forgetfulness, only memory is only probed, price claiming involved. Part of each story, reported to hurry, each line with wooly how. All directions knitted to be, combed from clatters of aunty forgery, machine pelting out clappers, gleaning threads of warmth as paragraph. Salman tone is invented, partially to carry. No word had width that wasn't encouraged, meant parsley sauce of pass it on, taken for granted or driven home. Tending language of Latin to run, meeting the girl from book upon. Present wheres of before, second nature applying feature. Example and modern fable, a recent crop of sport, somehow unbeaten with taking on rules, news strains are all impatient. slow wake of tower's encouragement, sizing catastrophe with impeding laws of freedom buzz, being sickly to interest of syllable corns. Pert crease of loud noise, afterwards damp moss. Anyone big fat blubbery lady from big fat blubbery lady. Hoovers to phones, danger queens of waking sleep. Settle impatience with nods to weep, using assassination habits as recognition seams, the chances are always spent by twit with fumble rent, biding days with ghostly ways, more alive with mischief than with grief. patience of cost stowed in rob caste, rogues with fags and clean toilets, goons glue maverick. sympathies disdained as rival doctors, all fools as danger inebriates. Set apart as glorious chart, un rhythmic to height of scale, having gone to sleep inside a whale. curious guilt of numb deceit, playing nearly bad to won't retreat. Tank of camp set, wondering where the rods are gifts. Lady with non pointer, no point. shut speak of everyone's leak, fitting the coins of drum rules, whatever filters oils, and freeze of goodwill perched about what it can impale. Late greatness of seizing lostness, honing in on wrong voice. Idiot with wrong hand, but swap fact to in command. bogey dumps of worn stumps, frilly pain of treat me better, treat men said men to me, N to the blubbery lady. What does position have to do with life when signature is the curled wife. Things with rings for the temper, temporary proceeds. Rinse brief for dropping the leg, chilling retreat with a cough for a hug. hungriness of fearlessness, sniffing out and concluding to policy. better unsaid, until the lawyers are. Pokey screen with rude probe, oddly advert sucking hose. interest fixing the shaft of taxing, giving meddler appropriate toy. All day employ, folding and reworking and huddling towards feeds, wondering if day shall bring a technical understanding to wishes about obliterating chance with polite vice. Trueness of keeping grimace, tense times to daily fitness, relax at one with rehash, until next lay by of harpoon. Hone in on machine thing, antic social reckoning. warped with crush enveloping, munching flavour of buoyant slits of comparison, rough. Flirt lights of carriage rights, buttoned to tulips, creepy padlock with heavy warlock, suddenly having to bin the plan. Having life minutely slight, set next jerk. toyed down from spilling proceeds, shares of demons conclusive and sickly. Flinch of reflex synch, easiness of sanity. Hardness a special depravity, pens ball in abacus. Bean count alien rise, jumper render complex ties. crash things that solids concern. Revolution frazzle intern. Displace gain sting, slut hop ecstatic signs. Interim composure, written off false. snuff without a family. Complaint bio shrink back up with wine. Proper frustration joining compendium, wondering on exterminate sieges of heroic worries. Is that ever was. Sorry miffed and then resilient. Move on reliant upon safe siege. Blankness draw true picture. Stick to mixy Bisto tunes, dues of national heroism. one person with full composition. one queen with a crown. court neither and supply. Dissolve chance with snapping the cards of traverse restrained. no ambition about peaceful inflation, bowed with back rods of love darts, pocket pouches of trouser forages, decline to fondle. glowering muddle. What if the goods propose, healthy peaches pointing toes. Refrains to naughty lanes, wondering on what comment is. Muffs and silly huffs, getting on. rude turn to pretend. there goes left bend. Strand admired in camouflage of landscape. Onset reception cloud, bristling bark richer colour, spatter neutrality of solemn wash down, funny lowered with atmosphere. clung rings of rainbows, infused lights of pulling drawers, places of glee in gold, mimic hump soggy plaster. Times reinstate conductor, promise officiator with effective clean bream. inculcator moo, there was a pause. qualified balled the wire to orbit load. Paths of real planets, collisions of lawlessness eject. Self respect of pity to rule, having but contrasting tools. Carry out things of people plots, friending up a heaven trot. One day at present be. Obstruct, reprieve and flick with gust. hip to hilt bride, sulk boy without a ride. button concession restriction. Pulling through conviction. Smart carpets, mosaics of roman delights. Pummel fancy mrs Nancy, loved to bits. Ripples and know hows. angry thing about floods, gates of thighs and nipple tassels. Dispensation soiled rules. coy further a poor prick, set back Rapunzel, baleful soul. House worshipful malice, contend to grow hair. Stalk fetch and caught, dismembered rhyme turn burn. phrase made with icing. Sugar layer of arts, poking fun. Bandwagon jettison, lob compensation to foster, good teas to wild cheese and mice in furs. set up to put upon, gain cook's custom. Find soul and fill a hole, landmarks to golfers or pimps. abuse feet of space. fill haste and change direction. intuitive slave to annoy. Minge of positive care. Grass a dandy, cap on head, mowing and clipping sea of the red. Greenaway a bowling sphere. shape nothing to win. Sorry cursory norm, imbue a heckler with a selfish brother, parting is a bad view. optimist unsaid to untrue, physiology of appeal. Sometimes boredom tease exhumes. no matter from beginnings. Fluff cushion and constitution, faith with beholding goods. tear duct of ticklish prongs, lately wrong required of needs. Ghoulish brain the reed, tell back stitch that wound up. Stake of voluntary silliness. Flu in doused woods of working coppice, flourish stoke the fires. Blindfolds and high wires. Whoever said slaves were menial taskers. nature subservient swig on liberties. Moan without saying, only signaling. Letter exchange bling. E become the rim. Attractive knighthood, course of settling required. Tower dice surrender, displace to hand. Dry port fleece respite. Subsequent wrap, time dance less talk. Policy spare secrecy, sided with three to a blackberry. Wide mouth cherry from glass house. squeeze through entry crates of eighty eights. Track sand banned, exhibit Hogarth to the lost projector, bawdier vision than current. flow encourage allocation. Only banter. plume glean mystery ten, skittle set among. Lord and advantage. Level wave to Biggles. peasantry seals of conceding. Slash tunes of serious longing, passages of relative tonging. Flap door rival curve, blobs and elders, muse on powder porters, fit dignity with elaborate chess. Concession fend boredom and entertainment. House of Keith, prunes of crew devolve. rescue plan in operation. islander flush gravity of sworn of dream. Beautiful cold. Spanish spat pane. Burn getaway with dribbler camel. what end process for sparking up and drugging on, being nicknamed. prig with bug to bear, praise prize. Meddle wound to wield, funnel mood exchanged. wonder love bear witness, drug it with permissive exclusiveness. Bland evade quiet part, tune volume, whizz on approaches and departures of relative belief. stick to a human pattern. Even though is only a mad station. reluctance conjoined, perform a required filters, faith gasp and rasp. pleasant expose and return feeds, spare highs to come what may. Side car parasite, attend speed flight. legal refer sip. Simon says with light keys, inner chasing guardians, pricks of homes as quarters. Ruffle discipline stop. Further a boob trap, silicone hem with chesty friend, torture with milk appeal, look squashy on page three. Touch a chameleon with hot rays, empower warmth escaping days. rhythm of escaping from distance. Completely apart with phrases, tie strings to foreign stories in the subdued state of bet and poor. Undoing nearly gold, brass with sheer eyes. having the core peeled. Mistress wench to crowns of value. weighing desperation with indulgence, un tucking. sustain bores of verbal lesions, qualify with daily conduct. Grow the grade of how to continue. Express foul play, strange to interject. Become understanding, either with a science of internal collection, mind the arts withdraw the cups, fill knowing for things that are. rest gets tar, dispensed conscience, presume to take reigns. Afloat net gains, shroud to princess. Sequence mends, worry on the composition. Objective gardens grow themselves, bee swarms and gum boots. compliments to issue, the partnership of place and blooms. Deep parts of owing to try, growing hair. Belonging and arrogant care, wedding aisle peripherals. assembly is terminal gazes, spent with blinks and dabs, and wit coughs, previous orders. Brilliance to please, as discerned ways, cajoling thing with bitchy good. Clearing part for resumptive start, cover of a handicap. true liar admire, feisty about served grade. Ignorant overplayed, result of a bullied wand. Falter with whatever, hook led to close perch. Brown in gloomy mulch, duck weed flat line grow suspense. noticeably poor, affordable flaw, intermingling with a notices to fashions. Times times layers of going and removing, ever arriving. Instance for laughs absolving, cutting the playing stem of understanding, curb under flecked reward, throttling dawns with tour inspections. conduct not commit, window scrabbler with a pressed nose. Knowing better but oblivious to the convoy. Everything is held up behind the expulsion. to find Just cheer up! Woo a pony catch, naughty thing. Don't throw rubbish born again. At last with tears of enormous consequence, slide mud on mountains. disembowel performance properly asserted. It was good to be apart, conclusion washing. Cover face with shared ices, use preservation. Although perplexity scratches, tits work round clearances. Decide to spend then timber amend, necking in the breakthrough. import go lightly, trounce with density. wedge a size for pounding heart, distance of completion of learn. Less substance to rocket fuel, discharge to effect. Complacency are round moods of drifting after rowing. dip design to stiffen oar, welling calm to butterflies. Observed the cabbage patch of go and fetch, tails of providers. Optimist deserter, wise avoid the choice. one look news hypotenuse. Resilient occasion of shared conundrum, civil prompt the host. use to light roast, unending change in questions. Hoppit same as pairs of robins, dirt aside in bracket. Footnote termite, castles of hot climates. rollick and chaffinch, hand and light stand. All manners of wrens, foreign for pastimes. Make up marge of poetry discharge, using against the harsh sledge, fitting quotes with stop quotes, days of lithe dizziness, being no part to a guillotine, chit meeting black taunt with silent owls. Part scares of mischievous wants, leaking and wielding. Insistence rules with crack aside cool, sincerity with spare parts, coining conclusivity with rearranged, only ten minutes before mantra of scenic composure, gig theme to general emulsion. Cans of skies and tunes calling, singing scales of vertical limbs. forward charts of notes, lined to read a single band. Gauguin distance expired trove. Wonder that love is told.

www.ingramcontent.com/pod-product-compliance
Lightning Source LLC
Chambersburg PA
CBHW071437080526
44587CB00014B/1891
9781910125946